Testimonials for Suzanne Venker:

"A voice in the wilderness...."

"You have massively impacted the way I see and deal with men. Because of you, I started dating with a clear goal in mind (marriage and children) and also with discipline. At twenty-five, this led me to my now boyfriend who soon will be my fiancé, husband, and hopefully father of my children. Thank you from the bottom of my soul for the enlightening and truthful work that you share with the world!"

"As a recovering feminist, the detoxing from such a harmful message and brainwashing so prevalent in our culture is a long process. Suzanne challenges the narratives and provides practical tools to live the alternative, which is a life that is more in line with our biology and what most of us actually desire. Keep up the good work!" —A reader

"Thank you, Suzanne, for being courageous to speak out against the mainstream agenda that was hurting and confusing me." —Daniela

"I wish I would have come across this twenty years ago when I was younger and really struggling to understand roles in relationships. I am so happy to have found it now so I can apply this advice to my current relationship. Thank you, Suzanne!"

"I almost failed miserably at marriage and parenthood because of the lies of the feminist movement. Suzanne is real. And smart. She sheds the light and the truth on what is most important in life: love, companionship, and connection." —Tiffany

"As a twenty-two-year-old woman in her senior year of college, I have been craving the message and information Suzanne has been putting out. Thank you, Suzanne, for putting age-old knowledge we have somehow forgotten back into our society so young women like me who hadn't heard much of it can learn from it and be better women and partners for our men." —Lorene

"I love sharing [Suzanne] with jaded lonely girlfriends, lol." —Annie

"Opened my eyes to realize how much of our 'junk food' culture has trickled into my life and how to fight back!" —MD Mom

"The world and my own mother haven't spoken to me about any of this. Schools and the media taught me that career comes first and that I would be happy even without getting married and not having children. I find this extremely harmful, especially for women. I thought what I was feeling wasn't quite normal until I found your work. Thank you sooo much, Suzanne!" — Lily from Australia

"I love, love, love the work you do. It's SO important. You are a true culture warrior." — Alyssa

"You. Are. Brilliant." — Alexis

"You are like the unofficial 'Internet Mom' who has the wisdom and experience to help guide us through problems. I often find myself going on walks and listening to 20 minutes of Suzanne Venker and feel clearer and calmer afterwards." — Shiva

"Best advice EVER!" — Katie

"Suzanne Venker is filled with a ton of wisdom. Younger ladies & men can learn so much from her. Her videos are like chapters in dating courses." — Olayinka

"Solid advice for people in an actual good quality marriage. [Suzanne Venker is] pretty much at the top-of-the-pile for information regarding this sort of thing." — Craig

Also by Suzanne Venker

The Alpha Female's Guide to Men and Marriage:
How Love Works

Women Who Win at Love:
How to Build a Relationship That Lasts

The Two-Income Trap:
Why Parents Are Choosing to Stay Home

HOW TO GET HITCHED (and Stay Hitched)

A **12-Step Program** for **Marriage-Minded** Women

Suzanne Venker

Post Hill
PRESS

A POST HILL PRESS BOOK
ISBN: 978-1-63758-052-3
ISBN (eBook): 978-1-63758-053-0

How to Get Hitched (and Stay Hitched):
A 12-Step Program for Marriage-Minded Women
© 2021 by Suzanne Venker
All Rights Reserved

Post Hill Press
New York • Nashville
posthillpress.com

Published in the United States of America
1 2 3 4 5 6 7 8 9 10

*NOTE: This book is an updated and revised version of the original book, with new material added.

for Emma, who's been detoxed
since the day she was born

And as always, to my husband Bill, whose support and
encouragement of my work has been unwavering since
day one. You're the best husband a girl could ever have.

CONTENTS

Just because everything is different doesn't mean anything has changed.
—Irene Peter

INTRODUCTION

DETOX

I first wrote this book some ten years ago now, and I find it mind-boggling how much more strained the relationship between the sexes has become since then. Modern marriage is a mess—as a coach, I see it every day—and traditional dating is dead. Men and women have never been more in the dark about to how to build a relationship that lasts.

There are many reasons for this sad state of affairs, some of which I cover in this book. But rather than focus on the why, I want to focus on helping *you* rise above the fray so you can succeed in life and in love.

To begin, I must apologize on behalf of your mothers and mentors. Your generation got seriously screwed.

You may have heard this argument before with respect to the debt your generation was encouraged to accrue, but that's only part of it. Equally significant, more significant actually, are matters of the heart.

Many of you are products of divorces and remarriages and come-and-go love. From your vantage point, relationships don't last. Even if that isn't the case, even your parents *are* married, almost no young woman today is raised to grow up and get married—and you certainly weren't taught *how* to love a man, the way your grand-mother likely was. If anything, you were taught to disassociate from men and to depend entirely on yourself for everything—as if men have nothing to offer.

This attitude you've been groomed to harbor is the reason you have yet to be successful in love. You've been mentally preparing for your relationships to go wrong because you've had no modeling or tutoring for how to get it right.

How to Get Hitched seeks to change that, and I wrote it for two specific groups of women: twenty-somethings who feel out of step for wanting to get married and have kids sooner rather than later, and thirty-somethings who are still single but wish they weren't.

You are not the problem. Society is.

How could you *not* be struggling? Unlike every other genera-tion in history, yours was taught to postpone marriage indefinitely or to ignore it altogether, as though having a happy marriage and family were unrelated to your happiness and well-being. As though it were a nice idea, or a possible accompaniment, to an otherwise satisfying life.

This message has been so strong for so long that it's now chic to be single. "Living alone comports with modern values. It promotes freedom, personal control, and self-realization—all prized aspects of contemporary life," wrote Eric Klinenberg, author of *Flying Solo*.[1]

But if flying solo is so great, why are online dating sites a *bil-lion* dollar industry, replete with clients looking to get hitched?

Sure, being single can be fun—for a while. But most people don't want to stay single forever. Men and women are irrevocably drawn together. Since the beginning of time, this attraction has been the driving force of our survival as a species and has almost always resulted in marriage.

Not anymore.

This is in large part due to the fact that the modern generation has had zero guidance on how to date, let alone on how to be married. Young women, in particular, aren't supposed to have marriage on their minds at all. They're supposed to pursue an education and career as if those two things alone are their *raison d'etre* and there's nothing else in life to consider.

And then there are the women who *have* been married but who are now divorced and back on the dating market. Many of these women are at a loss, too, although their circumstances differ somewhat from the younger set.

But regardless of age, the fact remains that there's an art to finding love and to sustaining it. It is a skill that depends upon a mindset, or set of beliefs, about men and marriage—and about what our role in a relationship with a man should be.

Unfortunately, women have been besieged with our culture's anti-male, anti-marriage narrative since the day they were born. Moreover, their mothers have given them terrible advice. So of course you're shooting blanks!

How to Get Hitched is designed to do two things: explain *why* you're struggling in love—hint: it's because you've been conditioned to think in a way that undermines your success in this realm— and deprogram you from the lies you've been fed. It's about why you're still single and how to change the way you think so you're not single anymore.

But this next part is very important. Despite the title, *How to Get Hitched* is less about finding a man and more about finding *you*. It's about what you really want vs. what you're told you should want, and it's about what is true of men and marriage versus what you believe to be true.

The first order of business is to recognize that the culture is your enemy. It is actively working against you every step of the way by selling bogus messages about life and love, like the idea that you shouldn't "settle" for anything less. than the best. But you are far from perfect. So why should your man be?

You'll also need to change your views on equality. Why? Because you've been sold a script about sex and gender roles that's ruining your ability to find lasting love.

For instance, you've been told you can have sex just like a man: without getting attached. But as actress Lena Dunham told Frank Bruni of *The New York Times*, this cultural expectation conflicts with human nature.

"I heard so many of my friends saying, 'Why can't I have sex and feel nothing?' It was amazing: that this was the new goal. There's a biological reason why women feel about sex the way *they* do and why men feel about sex the way they do. It's not as simple as divesting yourself of your gender roles."[2]

Indeed it isn't. But today's marriage-minded woman is up against a narrative that suggests moving in and out of hookups and quasi-committed relationships is somehow superior to the security of being in a real relationship in which marriage is the goal.

Hanna Rosin, author of *The End of Men: And the Rise of Women*, describes the new ethos this way: "Thanks to the sexual revolution, [women] can have relationships—and maybe some drama—through their twenties and early thirties and not get tied down with a husband and babies. If the price is a little more heartache, so be it. These days women have a lot more important things on their horizon."[3]

How on earth can women find lasting love when they've absorbed this elitist, self-serving crap since the day they were born?

Ms. Rosin is wrong. The price of the sexual revolution is not "a little more heartache." It's a boatload. For most women, at their core, nothing is more important than finding Mr. Right. Nothing.

But this massively misguided view of sex and relationships is the only frame of reference women have today when it comes to the most important part of their lives. And what have they learned?

That women and men are "equal," as in *the same*.

That is a lie. Being equal in worth, or value, is not the same thing as being identical, interchangeable beings. Men and women are, in fact, nothing alike when it comes to their needs, their desires, and their behaviors.

For example, it will surprise many women to know that who earns what in a marriage matters. Men are providers and protectors by nature; they are biologically wired to produce on behalf of their families in order to feel useful and whole.

Marriage-minded women work for different reasons. If they do so after they've had children, it's either a result of financial need (from having made poor decisions early on under the misguided notion they'd always be in the workforce), or if they're married to a strong breadwinner, out of a desire for autonomy. *Married mothers do not work out of a desire to provide for their man.* Being the primary breadwinner does not embolden wives the way it does husbands. On the contrary, it causes most women to become resentful and stressed out, and they eventually *lose* the desire they once felt for their man.

This doesn't happen when the sexes are reversed.

That's because women long to feel safe and cared for, emotionally and financially, by the man in their lives—that is in part where their sexual desire stems from. If a woman feels she can't depend on her man, the relationship becomes more maternal in nature. Over time, the marriage—and certainly the sex—breaks down.

Another big difference is that men do not parent their children in the same way women do, nor do men manage the home front in the same way women do. Men, as a rule, are less invested in the details of running a home. It is therefore unreasonable to expect them to do things at home the same way women do.

You will learn more about these differences in the coming pages. In the meantime, it is important to realize that at the core of the disconnection between the sexes is a massive attitude shift—away from love and family, toward a life focused exclusively on the self. And then we wonder why millions of women are on antidepressants.

I've personally heard more than one parent tell me their daughters say they're never getting married. That isn't surprising—look at their role models. As the caption on a cover story of *Boston Magazine*, entitled "Single by Choice," reads, "This is Terri. She's successful, happy, and at 38, just fine with never getting married. Ever."[4]

But most of these daughters—not all, but most—who are so adamantly opposed to marriage now will wake up from their fog one day. They will, as we say, grow up. And when they do, they will be despondent about having harbored such views. Because humans aren't, as it happens, designed to live alone. It may be chic to pretend otherwise, but that doesn't make it true. Smoking was once chic, too, and look how that turned out.

At the end of the day, it is fear that's driving these new attitudes and behaviors. Women *want* to find love; they just don't know how. They consistently ask where the good men have gone and don't realize it is women who shooed men away by competing with them rather than loving them.

Men don't want to be married to another version of themselves; they want something different. They want the feminine, the very thing women have been groomed to reject.

You have no idea how much power there is in the feminine; men gravitate toward it like bees to honey. And the good news is, your femininity is lying dormant inside you, ready for you to grab it at any time.

Femininity softens the masculine and brings out the best in men. Problem is, you've been taught to believe that being a woman—being soft, nurturing, kind—means being weak or being *less than* a man. That was another lie. (Oh, there are so many!)

This will be hard to hear, but it was women's rejection of *themselves* as God (or nature, if you prefer) made them that has unknowingly created the environment we're now in.

Men will almost always respond to what women command. If your standards are low, men will go low. If your standards are high, men will go high. That's the power you wield as a woman.

All of which is to say this: If you want to navigate the dating scene, find Mr. Right, and settle down in a culture that's hell bent on steering you in a different direction, you have only one option.

A detox.

A detox, you probably know, is the process an addict goes through when he wants to rid himself of toxins that have invaded his body. When it comes to sex and relationships, men and marriage, work and family, our culture is toxic. This toxicity is so pervasive, in fact, you've become numb to it. You probably don't even see it.

Sadly, many women will allow this poison to invade their minds and hearts and even ruin their lives. *But you don't have to.*

There are three steps involved in any detox:

1. Recognize the problem.

2. Rid your body of the toxins.

3. Give your body the healthy nutrients it craves.

In other words, you must *recondition your brain* to think about men and marriage in a way that contradicts everything you've been taught since the day you were born.

A tall order? Yes. But it can be done.

And I will help you.

It had seeped into their minds like intravenous saline into the arm of an unconscious patient. They were feminists without knowing it.
—Danielle Crittenden

PART ONE

4 LIES THE CULTURE TELLS

CHAPTER 1

MARRIAGE + MOTHERHOOD = JAIL

Whenever I talk to women in their twenties and thirties about feminism, it usually falls on deaf ears. To most of them, feminism was just some movement where women burned their bras and fought for women's rights. The details escape them. But what these women do know, or *think* they know, is that they owe their lives to the feminists who came before them. After all, that's what they've been told over and over and over again.

What would it mean for you to learn this isn't true?

Feminism is not what you think it is. Or, at least, it's no longer what it once was. Regardless of its initial intent or even its inevitability, it is, at its core, a radical movement and ideology.

Of course, it has never been billed as such. Rather, it is sold as something any enlightened human being, male or female, should embrace. The assumption is that, if it weren't for feminists, women in America would be second-class citizens. They'd be stuck in secretarial jobs or at home doing the grunt work of caring for the house and kids while men got to go out and lead exciting lives in the marketplace.

Putting aside for the moment that this narrative glorifies wage labor (most men do not view their jobs as liberating), most people do not have careers—they have jobs. And what separates careers from jobs is that careers are *all-consuming*. A career may start out new and exciting, but the higher you climb and the more money you make, the more demanding it becomes. Until one day, your career owns you. You realize you have no life outside of it.

The greatest travesty of it all is that women now associate their self-worth, or value, with what it is they *do*—rather than with who it is they *are*. Far from having been liberated, women are trapped by the workforce and have become chronically unhappy and dissatisfied. Professionally, they're kicking ass. But their careers aren't doing what they were told they would do.

They aren't filling them up.

Have you ever read the Hans Christian Andersen story *The Emperor's New Clothes*? I'm always reminded of it when I think about feminism's influence on society and what would happen if people were privy to the facts.

A vain emperor who cares only about his appearance hires two tailors who are, in fact, swindlers. They promise the emperor the finest clothes, made from a fabric that's invisible to those too dense to see it. The emperor can't see the cloth himself but pretends he can out of fear of appearing stupid. When the swindlers finish making the suit, the emperor marches in procession before his subjects, who play along with the pretense.

Suddenly, a child in the crowd, too young to understand the desirability of keeping up the pretense, shouts that the emperor is wearing nothing at all! Then the crowd admits they don't see anything either. The emperor cringes with embarrassment, but continues with the procession—vowing never to be swindled again.

Feminists, in effect, are swindlers. Their agenda is made up of, well, not *nothing* exactly, but bits and pieces of truth that are sewn together in such a way that the end result is a fabrication that sounds perfectly reasonable.

A great example is equal pay for equal work. Sounds benign, doesn't it? Who *wouldn't* believe in getting paid for work you've actually performed? But that's just it: Women don't make as much as men precisely because they *don't* work the same number of hours as men. Women continue to take years off the job to care for their children, or their aging parents, or to simply live a more balanced life. They also don't take the unpleasant or dangerous jobs men do, which pay more. Feminists leave that part out.

The media, for example, routinely claim that most mothers today are "working mothers." But they don't define this term. Instead, they lump all mothers who bring home *any income at all* as "working mothers"—even though there's a clear distinction between mothers who work sixty or eighty hours a week while their toddlers are in other's care, and mothers who work twenty hours a week while their older children are in school.

That's why feminists are swindlers: they take a grain of truth and spin the hell out of it.

Many people also associate feminism with the right to vote, since feminists claimed their movement was simply a continuation of the 19th century suffragettes' fight for the female vote. By piggybacking off this earlier movement, feminism is now classified as first-, second-, or third-wave feminism. The first wave is associated with the female vote, the second wave is associated with the sexual revolution, and the third (and even fourth) wave are so radical they've thrown out the fact that there are only two genders.

In reality, second-wave feminists had little in common with the suffragettes, who were anti-abortion. But in putting the two movements together, by claiming women in America are oppressed by men in the same way many blacks were once oppressed by some whites, it was easy for feminists to gain traction. After all, any thinking person believes women should vote, and any sane person believes slavery is evil. Ergo, "equal rights for women" must be a good thing, too.

But any serious study of feminism—there are a copious number of books, articles, and films if you're interested—reveals startling truths and commonalities among its leaders. For instance, almost every feminist leader had a dysfunctional upbringing, fraught with emotional abuse or neglect—and feminists (understandably) internalized this dysfunction as children. Here's a direct quote from Gloria Steinem: "I didn't understand the degree to which my response has been magnetized by things that had happened to me before—and I think that realization came out of being depressed."[5]

When women like Steinem grew up, they displaced their pain onto society. Instead of putting their personal stories in context by realizing their mothers' unhappiness was their own to contend with, they concluded their mothers weren't to blame for their problems. They figured that if society had functioned the way it was supposed to in the first place—with men and women as interchangeable sexes, each being interested and capable of doing the same work—their mothers would have been happy.

Harboring this attitude allows feminists to resent their mothers less and to hate men and society more. See how it works?

As to the changes that have occurred with gender roles, it's true more women run companies today and more fathers change diapers—which is all well and good. It is also true that feminism may have helped force this along. But it was ultimately an *inevitable* phenomenon, as technological changes continued to provide opportunities for women that didn't exist before.

In almost every era, technology provided women with the means to an easier life. In the 1940s, it was the washing machine; in the 1960s, it was the birth control pill; in the 1990s, it was the Internet. (Other inventions included the sewing machine, the frozen food process, the automobile, etc.) All of these advancements—which were created by *men*, I might add—made life at home far less taxing.

It was the combination of birth control, along with technology and labor-saving devices, that ultimately liberated women from the taxing nature of round-the-clock housework and childcare. They gave women what they've always craved: time. The more time women had, the more they were able to enter the workforce. And the more women joined the workforce, the more husbands started taking on an active role at home.

Of course, these changes haven't amounted to a full-scale gender role reversal because human nature doesn't change. After all this time, women still choose the caregiving professions (nursing, teaching, etc.) at a significantly higher rate than men; and men still choose the physical and dangerous jobs (climbing trees and tall buildings, going into dark alleys with guns to confront bad guys) far more than women. And much to the dismay of our current administration, which is actively working to change this, women also still choose to be their children's primary caregivers, while men choose to be their families' primary breadwinners.

I'm sure you've also heard over and over again that mothers today "have" to work. That may sometimes be the case, but the impetus for the mass exodus of mothers from the home was not a need for more money. It was the result of the relentless status degradation of the at-home mother. Women were conditioned to believe that by staying home to raise a family their lives would be rendered meaningless. They'd "lose themselves" in the process.

In fact, the shift away from mothers at home toward mothers at work is part and parcel of a larger cultural shift—away from family and onto the self, away from sacrifice and toward materialism. Today, women map out their lives according to this new set of values—such as making financial decisions based on two incomes—and then get "stuck" later on when they realize they want to stay home with their kids.

That's not the same thing as "having" to work, as though someone or something thrust the situation upon them—like when my grandmother had to go to work after my grandfather was laid off during the Depression. We simply created a new economic model. The "having to work" argument doesn't even make sense. As a nation we used to be much poorer, and most mothers were home!

That is not to say there aren't mothers in the workforce who need to be there—that 41 percent of mothers in this country are unmarried is evidence enough—but this doesn't make the facts about how we got here any less true. In the past, being a wife and mother was a noble vocation. In modern America, marriage + motherhood = jail.

"I'd always had this feeling that if you got married, it was like the end of who you were,"[6] Sandra Bullock told Barbara Walters in a March 2010 interview. This attitude is now commonplace. Even men have jumped on board.

The saddest part of the whole thing is that lasting love has been all the more elusive since the push for faux equality began. Feminists assured women their efforts would result in more satisfying, equitable marriages—but that has not happened. Instead, one of three things happens.

1. Women postpone marriage indefinitely and move in and out of intense romantic relationships, often even

living with their boyfriends. Eventually, their clocks start ticking and many decide they better hurry up and get married to provide a stable home for their yet-to-be-born children. Trouble is, they can't find a man who's worthy of marrying or who's willing to commit.

2. Marriage becomes a competitive sport. The complementary nature of marriage—in which two people work together, as interdependent agents, toward the same goal but with an appreciation for the unique qualities each gender brings to the table—has been obliterated. Today, husbands and wives are locked in a battle about who does more on the home front and how they're going to get everything done. That's not marriage. That's war.

3. No-fault divorce, which feminists support since women—who initiate two-thirds of all divorces—must be "happy" at all costs, makes ending one's marriage a piece of cake. Just check the "irreconcilable differences" box, and off you go.

So, I'll ask you: Do you still think women are indebted to feminism?

CHAPTER 2

"NEVER DEPEND ON A MAN"

Of all the messages your generation has adopted, the most egregious is the one many of your mothers passed on: "Never depend on a man." The women who pounded this home did so for one reason: because their own relationships with men—either their fathers or their husbands, sometimes both—were fraught with emotional turmoil. When this happens, feminism becomes a convenient way to stay mad at the entire male population. Sadly, many mothers then pass this damaging mindset on to their daughters.

Here's what you need to ask yourself. Was your mother *truly* a victim of her circumstances? Was her father or her husband—your grandfather or your father—really a bad guy?

That's certainly possible. But if your mother's marriage to your father failed, it's *just as possible* your mother didn't do her part to create a strong marriage. And if she was at heart an unhappy woman, it's also just as possible her life plans got derailed because of poor choices she made along the way.

How you sort all of this out is crucial because it will put your mother's advice in context. You may determine, for example, that she's not a happy woman or that she's victim-oriented by nature. If that's the case, I'm afraid her advice isn't going to help you. What you need to do is forget all the negative vibes she sent forth about men, marriage, and motherhood. No matter how hard it is, accept that your mother doesn't have the answers you're looking for.

The truth is, the previous generation of American mothers did their daughters a great disservice. They were wrong to tell their daughters to never rely on a man and to be independent their entire lives instead—making all their own money, never staying home with kids, and expecting nothing from anyone. Harboring this attitude undermines a marriage before it even gets off the ground.

It's time to put the message that pursuing a career is the only way a mother can retain her identity in the trash, where it belongs. Getting married and having a family doesn't chip away at a woman's (or a man's) identity. It shapes it.

As for not being able to depend on a man, that just isn't true. Unless you made an exceptionally bad choice, like marrying a former convict from the backwoods, this is not going to be your fate. Most men are much more dependable than you've been led to believe.

Men also aren't, as a rule, threatened by a woman with power. *They only care if and when this power gets used against them or the marriage.* There's nothing wrong with being successful in the marketplace; where women get into trouble is when they bring their empowered selves home.

Marriage isn't a power struggle; it's a team effort. Unless your husband is a Neanderthal—in which case, why'd you marry him in the first place?—he's not the least bit interested in seizing your identity. Most men don't want a doormat for a wife.

One of the greatest ironies of the feminist claim that women live in a patriarchy in which men want to hold women down and back is that it never even occurs to the average husband to do this. In most cases, all that energy women spend putting up a force-field is for naught.

It's true that *children* curtail your independence; babies are totally dependent creatures. But life is about trade-offs. You can't have everything you want, exactly the way you want it, all the time. When you gain in one area, you lose in another. What goes up must come down. This is a law of physics you can't do anything about.

If you really want to feel liberated, try accepting this truism rather than fighting against it. Now *that's* freedom.

Here's something else that may surprise you. Most women find they *want* to stay home with their babies when they become mothers, despite the culture pulling them in the other direction. It's human nature to want to care for your own children.

What that means, then, is that the smart thing to do when mapping out your future is to assume the *opposite* of what your mother told you. Assume you *will* want, and need, to depend on your husband at some point in time. His job will allow you to care for your children, for however long you choose to, without having to worry about producing an income. It's a wonderful (and natural) give-and-take between husband and wife.

But you have to be open to it.

Of course, many couples switch things up—she works; he stays home—but most women want to take care of their children themselves, especially their babies. And most men would rather provide the means that allow their wives to do so.

Men have a vested interest in their children, too. Being products of divorce, many men today didn't have a mother at home and wish they had. Consequently, they would like their own children to have what they didn't have. But men have no voice in America. They can't ask, let alone expect, their wives to stay home. Not in a million years.

On the other side of the fence are the men who bought into feminist gobbledygook. They, too, have been pressured and cajoled into thinking educated women shouldn't "lower" themselves to depending on a man in order to take care of their babies, if only for a few years.

The unfortunate result of this cultural narrative is that many women today have to convince their husbands that staying home is the right thing to do. These women aren't just fighting their mothers and the culture.

They're fighting their own husbands! That we now have a country in which mothers have to *justify their desire to care for their own children* speaks volumes. It's tragic.

But it makes sense, doesn't it? After all, men were sold the same script women were. They, too, absorbed the message that women shouldn't depend on men. In their mind, since most men don't feel an innate desire to care for their babies around the clock, why would women? Men and women are the same!

Men have also been sold on the bogus idea that babies can thrive in daycare. In one article I wrote about the importance of staying home, a male commenter had this to say: "Education is a tough thing to waste, Suzanne, particularly when you've spent so much of your money, your parents [sic] money, (and with financial aid/grants) full-tuition paying students/taxpayer's money to get it. To then 'stay home' and 'raise children' after spending all that money, well, I could see why that would anger some people. I could see where some might call that a very selfish thing to do. I'm sorry if you can't see that."[7]

I find this mind-boggling. Is there anything in the world more self*less* than raising babies?

To be fair, this man's comment is unusual. Most men I hear from fully understand the social and economic value of parenting. Still, they don't feel comfortable asking their wives to stay home or talking about this topic in public. They know if they did, they'd be branded sexist. That these fathers just want what's best for their children doesn't matter. Simply *thinking* such a thing dubs a man a chauvinist.

What I don't want for you is to end up like those women in the magazines, the ones who are successful in their field but whose love lives and home lives are a mess. Working mothers blame employers, husbands, even God for why they can't find balance in their lives. But time is their real enemy.

These women bought into the myth that happiness and contentment lie outside the home, not inside. They bought into all that junk that a woman shouldn't have to cook for or take care of a man. Today's women are enlightened! They're men's equals! They don't have to do any of that stuff.

What a load of crap. Being a wife and a strong woman are not mutually exclusive. And cooking for a husband, or simply taking care of one's family, does not in any way diminish your value. Shocking as it seems, it's rather rewarding.

CHAPTER 3

SEX IS JUST SEX

If I were the gambling type, I'd put money on the fact that you know many women who've slept with more guys than they can count. I know I do.

I'm not sure how I managed to escape all that; I've just always viewed casual sex as a colossally stupid idea. Jordan Peterson sums it up perfectly: "People treat sex like it's casual. It's not. Sex is unbelievably complicated. It's dangerous. It involves emotions. It involves pregnancy. It involves illness. It involves betrayal. It reaches right down into the roots of someone. You don't play with something like that casually. Well, you can, but you'll pay for it."[8]

And yet, women have been told this behavior is somehow liberating. For years women have been assured that "hooking up," or having indiscriminate sex, demonstrates a woman's self-confidence and power.

Actually, it demonstrates the opposite. To willingly let countless men inside you proclaims how *little* you think of yourself and takes *away* your power.

When it comes to sexuality, American women have engaged in a massive social experiment, and the damage has been profound. Some learn the lesson about casual sex after a sordid night or two, while others don't begin to understand or even acknowledge the ramifications for years—when it's often too late.

What makes the message so insidious is that young women are prone to feeling insecure and are thus vulnerable to the idea that sleeping with a guy will make him more attached to her. But that is not how it works for men.

Indeed, the women my age who fell into that trap are mortified about their past behavior. And to those who feel otherwise, I would ask this: Are you going to suggest your daughters do the same thing? Or your sons, for that matter?

Not only are women encouraged to be promiscuous, they're told their libidos are the same as men's. That's an egregious lie. I found my favorite description of the male sex drive in the book *Letters to My Daughters* by political consultant Mary Matalin. In the book, she shares an anecdote from her mother, who once said to Mary, "Men would screw a snake if it would sit still long enough."[9]

I know, right? I couldn't stop laughing when I first read it. Don't take it literally—most men aren't that bad. It's just a funny take on what is undoubtedly the biggest difference between men and women. You could never turn that sentence around and say *women* would screw a snake if it would sit still long enough. The visual is preposterous! Sex just isn't a woman's primary M.O.

That doesn't mean women don't *enjoy* sex. It's just that what they need in this department is very different from what men need. Plus, women don't think about sex as often or in the same way as men do. According to neuropsychiatrist Louann Brizendine, author of *The Female Brain* and *The Male Brain*, sexual thoughts float through a man's brain every fifty-two seconds, on average, while a woman may think about sex only once a day.[10]

The reason women today *appear* obsessed with sex is twofold. First, all of us are saturated with sexual images and messages from the media. You'd think sex is the entire purpose of our existence. There's no perspective on the subject at all.

Second, women have been assured that, deep down, they really do enjoy sleeping around. Society just didn't allow women to express themselves in this manner until feminism came along to liberate them.

What bunk. Women are literally *made* to bond, and because of this are generally unable to separate sex from emotion. The whole "love 'em and leave 'em" thing just isn't a female practice—which is something that should be honored and respected, not minimized or ridiculed.

It used to be. People didn't know *why* women were different from men because the science wasn't there yet, but they knew it just the same. They knew it from experience, and they knew it in their gut.

Today we have proof. The female body, it turns out, is steeped in oxytocin and estrogen, two chemicals that together produce an environment ripe for attachment. Oxytocin, known primarily as the female reproductive hormone, is particularly relevant. Oxytocin causes a woman to bond with the person with whom she's intimately engaged. It also acts as a gauge to help her determine whether or not she should trust the person she's with.

Men have oxytocin, too, but a smaller amount. They're more favored with testosterone—which controls lust, not attachment. That's why women, not men, wait by the phone the next day after a one-night stand. That's why the movie *He's Just Not That Into You* wasn't titled *She's Just Not That Into You*. When a woman has sexual contact of any kind, it's an emotional experience whether she intends it to be or not. The moment touch occurs, oxytocin gets released and the attachment process begins.

It just doesn't happen the same way for men. Call it unfair, but there it is.

The truth is, being restrained, or cautious, with one's sexuality is where a woman's true power lies. Any woman can strut her stuff and sleep with the hottest guy in town—that's no big feat—but the woman who chooses not to stands out. To borrow a phrase from one of the sons on the hit 1970s TV series, *The Waltons*, "Who wants butterflies that fight to get into your net?"

Setting high standards for oneself garners not just self-respect but respect from others. There's nothing more attractive than a savvy woman who doesn't become jello in the presence of a hottie. If she likes a guy, she doesn't let him know it. Instead, she holds her cards close to her chest until she determines his intentions and character.

I don't say this stuff because I'm a prude. On the contrary, I'm very open about sex. I think sex is great. *But it has its place.* And that place is absolutely, definitely, not on the first date. Or the second, or the third. Smart sex occurs only within the context of a loving, monogamous relationship with a man who loves and respects you—and that takes time to build. If you skip this step, your man won't fully commit.

There's no question, of course, that modern women are more sexually savvy than their grandmothers were. But unlike their grandmothers, they know next to nothing about how to make a relationship work. That's because they've been taught that sexual restraint is a form of repression that represents an archaic social construct designed to hold women down.

That was the engine of the sexual revolution. Prior to the 1970s, Americans understood that men and women are different, not just physically but emotionally. Men honored women's femininity, not because they thought women were weaker or "less than" but because (ironically) they believed women were superior!

That may sound odd, but it's true. Women have always been viewed as moral agents, or a man's "better half." For years, this was a dominant theme in Hollywood films such as *It's a Wonderful Life* or *The African Queen*.

Men need women to steer them in a healthy sexual direction. From the moment a male comes out of the womb, who's responsible for civilizing them? Women. Women are the arbiters of male conduct. That's why we need women to act like women and not like men, sexually or otherwise.

This reminds me of one of my favorite exchanges. It took place in 1972, between journalist Lawrence E. Spivak and feminist icon Gloria Steinem on *Meet the Press*. Spivak said to Steinem, "You made a speech at the National Press Club in which you said, and I quote, 'Women are not taken seriously in this country. We're undervalued, ridiculed, or ignored by a society which consciously or unconsciously assumes the white male is the standard and the norm.' Now, what's your explanation for this serious state of affairs in view of the fact that males are virtually controlled and dominated by women from birth to puberty and often beyond that?"[11]

Steinem was genuinely stumped. Not being a mother herself, all she could say was that she didn't accept the premise of Spivak's statement. In other words, she thought males are not dominated by females. Ha! Ask my ten-year-old son, whose teachers are all female and who (in addition to his father) lives with his mother, sister, and grandmother. From the day males are born, their lives are undeniably dominated by women. Even single-parent homes are predominantly run by women.

While it may seem otherwise in today's day and age, I personally believe most men want to find a woman with whom they can settle down. But if women don't create an environment that's conducive to this goal, if they offer a smorgasbord of sex and even agree to live with their boyfriends with no commitment, men will delay marriage as long as possible. Men just aren't programmed to commit the way women are. They typically need to be brought to the table.

So where does this leave you, the marriage-minded woman? Well, there's no question the hookup culture makes it twice as difficult for women to find husbands. Men may be passing you by and going where they can get some action, and that's unfortunate.

But it's good news, too. It means you can weed out the guys who aren't ready for marriage from those who are. Because the guy who wants to just get laid isn't the kind of guy you want to marry anyway.

Whenever I think about today's films and television programs, where men and women take off their clothes at the end of their first date, I consider how totally devoid of romance and meaning it all is. I reflect on how sad it is that women have been so misled. I think about how women are cavorting around, pretending they want to screw a snake for the sake of pure pleasure, when what they really want is someone to love who will love them back forever. What a profound and beautiful gift that is.

And we totally dismiss it.

CHAPTER 4

CAREER SUCCESS WILL (AND SHOULD) DEFINE YOU

Let me guess. All the women in your life—your mother, your professors, your friends, your mentors—expect(ed) you to make a career the focus of your life. Marriage was rarely talked about; or if it did come up, it was looked upon as something so far in the future only a fool would spend time thinking about it. Is that about right?

The message to women is clear: career first, marriage later—much later. Maybe even not at all. If you want to be like everyone else, or heck, just be *normal*, you don't plan your life around being a wife and mother. No one does that.

Well, I did—and that's why my life worked out. I have a happy marriage, two great kids, and a booming career. None of this was happenstance; I made it happen. And you can, too.

I'm sorry you can't talk openly to your friends and family about your desire to get married and have kids. But I assure you, your friends who give no thought to marriage now will be running to the altar when their biological clocks start winding down.

Women have been taught to ignore their biological clocks until the final hour, the assumption being there will always be a pot of young men waiting for them when they're ready.

There won't be.

Marriage-minded men look for young, fertile women with whom to settle down. An older, career-focused woman with a long sexual history holds no allure to a man of high quality. Your mentors forgot to mention that part.

The older women who do find husbands also tend to suffer long, painful, and expensive procedures trying to conceive a child in unorthodox ways, after which they're expected not to savor the result but instead find "quality" child care and continue with life as it was before. What's liberating about any of that?

I'm reminded of a woman named Laurie Wagner, whom I wrote about in my book, *The Two-Income Trap*. She described her view of motherhood this way: "I had it all planned out: I'd birth Ruby, bond with her, and then resume life as I knew it, writing, working, reading, going to movies and restaurants. Ruby would be nearby, strapped on to me like some exotic appendage, delightful, lovely, and obedient, living my life with me. And then, one June, Ruby came."[12]

That's how your generation was taught to map out their lives: as though children are supposed to accommodate *you*, rather than you accommodating them. The average woman today postpones marriage and motherhood because she knows having a family will curtail her career plans. What no one tells her is how dramatically her life will change *for the better* once she becomes a mother. No one told her that this is when her life actually begins.

One of the most shocking discoveries is when women realize how much they love their babies and want to be with them. Some years ago I spoke with a woman who had quit her job as a nurse in the Navy to become a full-time mom. Her son was just over a year old at the time, and I asked her what had changed her mind about staying home with him. She said, "I just want to be with him. I got to thinking, 'What's the point of having children in the first place?'"

When I asked her why she hadn't thought she might feel this way beforehand, she said it never occurred to her to *not* go back to work. After all, there was a daycare center right across the street from where she worked, so she assumed everything would work out great. "But," she said, "no one ever told me how much I would miss him."

Women's priorities simply change when they have children. Not for the *worse*—for the better. In previous generations, women embraced this transformation and viewed motherhood as the beginning, not the end, of their lives. Today women view it as something to be postponed, something to worry about later, something that gets in the way of their better plans.

When my mother, who's now deceased, attended her graduate school reunion at Radcliffe, the former all-female sister institution of Harvard, one of her professors gave a lecture about work and family and said women would need to deal with children as an "intrusion" in their lives.

And so it is that women are surprised to find themselves consumed with maternal desire. When they finally do become mothers, many are shocked to discover that what they thought was important before they had children feels utterly irrelevant afterward. This is what marks the change in a woman's values, a change that becomes more amplified over the years.

That is why, in Part Two of this book, I've laid out a 12-step program designed to deprogram you from the lies the culture tells about sex, men, marriage, work, and family: so you can make smart decisions for the future you're likely to have.

Whom you choose to marry, and how that marriage fares, is *the single most important decision you'll ever make in your lifetime*. It will be the barometer of everything else you do. It is therefore critical you approach this decision without the clutter of social expectations. And of all the expectations of women today, the most significant—and destructive—is the notion that women can have everything they want all at the same time: a great marriage, a fabulous career, and a couple of impressive kiddos.

But as Anne-Marie Slaughter wrote in her wildly successful cover story in *The Atlantic* (July/August 2012), titled, "Why Women Still Can't Have It All," that is a lie. Slaughter's article hit a global nerve because millions of women know the truth about the promises of feminism. "For the remainder of my stint in Washington," wrote Slaughter, "I was increasingly aware that the feminist beliefs in which I had built my entire career were shifting under my feet."[13]

Indeed, feminism didn't help women 'have it all.' It *kept* women from having what they want most by insisting they focus solely on their careers while ignoring their desire for love and family. That's not having it all. That's having half.

Too many people don't realize what feminism did. It didn't just change Americans' understanding of sex and gender roles. *It changed the very meaning of life*. It took the spotlight off the things that matter—love, family, and a sense of place—and put it where it doesn't belong: on money, power, and status. It altered who we are as a people.

At the end of the day, it comes down to this question: What do you want? What do you *value*? Because no matter where you are in life, you can always pull a U-ey and start heading toward what really matters.

If what you want is some version of everything—meaningful work, a good marriage, and a healthy dose of motherhood and apple pie—you're in perfectly good company. That's what most of us want. And there's no reason you can't have it.

But first you must shift your priorities.

I know everything I'm writing contradicts what you've been told. And I know it must be difficult to accept that your mentors—perhaps even your own mother—have been, well . . . I was going to say misguided, but let's call it what it is: wrong.

But you'll have to do it. Because, as I think you already know, there's nothing empowering about moving in and out of countless romantic relationships, postponing marriage indefinitely, or pursuing careers with a verve that belies common sense.

There's *nothing* empowering about shacking up, ignoring your biological clock, refusing to depend on a husband (and thus feeling compelled to return to work after you give birth), or becoming a single mom. To be truly empowered, you're going to have to do a 180.

There's no other way.

Change your thoughts, and you change your world.
—Norman Vincent Peale

PART TWO

THE 12-STEP PROGRAM

LIVE AN EXAMINED LIFE

Now it's time to begin your detox. I hope you'll be able to enlist your friends in this 12-step program, but keep in mind it may be a while before they're ready. Some, of course, will never be ready.

But you *are*. So grab a glass of wine, put on some cozy socks, and get comfortable. We have a lot to cover.

At the end of the day, people live one of two lives: an examined life or an unexamined life. An unexamined life is when you move through the years mindlessly, not really thinking about what you're doing or why you're doing it, or even if you *like* doing it. You're just doing it, whatever "it" is, because that's what other people are doing—because that's what you think you're supposed to do. Or because, quite frankly, it's easier. Living an unexamined life means living a life someone else designed *for* you.

The examined life is different. The examined life is when you tune out the voices, sounds, and visuals in your midst and make important decisions based on what *you* want and on what *you* believe is right. More than anything, it means dismissing cultural trends that conflict with your core beliefs.

This is extremely hard to do, of course, which is why most people don't do it. But if you want to live an authentic life, it must be done. As Gordon MacDonald wrote *in Ordering Your Private World*, "Few of us can fully appreciate the terrible conspiracy of noise there is about us, noise that denies us the silence and solitude we need for this cultivation of the inner garden."[14]

Unfortunately, most of this "noise" today comes in the form of media. Earlier generations were fortunate in that they lived primarily with their own thoughts and with the thoughts of friends and family. We do not. Instead, the "conspiracy of noise" we endure 24/7 clouds our vision and impairs our judgment, pulling us away from our own beliefs and desires.

The only way to live an examined life is to avoid the chatter in your midst, which includes *any* media that sends a message that's counterproductive to your goal. And if you've picked up this book, we both know your goal is to get—and, presumably, to stay—married.

Which means there's going to be a helluva a lot of media you're going to have to ignore.

There's more. Once you remove the negative cultural messages (and I realize you won't be able do this entirely, unless you take up residence with the Amish), to ensure you don't get sucked back in you'll need to spend time with people who think the way you do and carve out some space from those who don't. That will be especially hard. But if you want to make smart choices for your future, you have no choice. Whom you surround yourself with matters.

I cannot stress enough the power of trends. Some are benign—like big hair in the 1980s—but some—such as promiscuity—are not. Either way, the trend becomes absorbed in the culture to such a degree that people feel compelled to jump on board, even if they'd rather not. Like I said, it's just easier and more comfortable to go along with the crowd.

That isn't *always* a bad thing, but it can be. Depends what the crowd is doing.

When it comes to making smart life decisions, particularly big ones, it is *essential* that you surround yourself with positive influences. The more you surround yourself with people or messages that support your goal, the more successful you will be in your mission.

As an example, suppose you wanted to lose a bunch of weight and had a choice between two doors you could open to help you accomplish your goal. Behind the first door is a roomful of obese people, and behind the second door is a roomful of strong, healthy, fit people—Dr. Oz types. Which door would you want to open? It's a no-brainer, isn't it? If you're serious about losing weight, you need to be around people who can help you get there.

The same is true with marriage.

To drive this point home, let's assume you weren't born when you were. Let's say you were born in the 1940s instead, when divorce was uncommon and when there was no such thing as the Internet. In this case, the influences in your life would be mainly friends and family, who are the people you'd see and hear from the most. Now let's also assume your parents were one of the few couples you knew who happened to be divorced. How might your beliefs about marriage be different?

You might be skeptical, given your parents' divorce, except presumably the rest of your family members—your aunts, uncles, cousins, etc.—*would* be married, as would your neighbors, thus providing you with a different model from the one you have at home. And since cable and on-demand television, or the Internet, wouldn't exist, you wouldn't be walloped every day with headlines and slogans that tell you this woman's getting a divorce or that woman's become a single mother by choice. Nor would you be exposed to programs like *Sex and the City* that promote casual sex, materialism, and a "You Go, Girl" attitude.

Instead, most of what you would see would be families that consist of married parents and their children.

The environment in which we're raised is critical to our ability to make smart choices. People are heavily influenced by what they see and hear around them. Whatever support and camaraderie we experience will significantly affect, for better or for worse, the decisions we make.

But alas, you were not born in the 1940s. In the world you know, sex and divorce are rampant, marriage is on the decline, and mass media is everywhere you look. That means you're privy to what everyone else is doing, or what it *looks* like everyone else is doing.

And the perception is that women everywhere are living carefree lives devoid of any responsibility. Other than their jobs, of course, and those are touted as glamorous, not laborious. This perception makes the average woman feel insecure about the kind of life she wants to build for herself. All of a sudden, getting married and having babies seems so . . . backward.

And the worst part is that the lives of the women we see in the media aren't even real. It's an illusion. You can't see the day-to-day reality of their lives, which is far from glamorous. Which means everyday women are making very real decisions about their very real lives based on something they absorb as real but isn't!

As a consumer of media, you're not supposed to be a passive observer when you watch those romantic comedies or read about the lives of Hollywood stars. You're not supposed to just watch the Lady Gagas of the world, or the women on *The View*, or even the folks on Food Network. You're supposed to *identify* with them.

This wouldn't be a problem if the women in the media represented, or even touted, the values most Americans share. But they don't. Most of the high-profile women we hear from on a regular basis are single, divorced, or hard-core working mothers with well-paid nannies. And these women, along with their colleagues, are responsible for framing the cultural debate. Here are just a few headlines of the past few years:

"Who Needs Marriage?" (*Time*, Nov. 18, 2010)

"The End of Men "(*The Atlantic*, July/Aug 2010)

"For Women, Is Home Really So Sweet?" (*The Wall Street Journal*, Feb. 18, 2012)

"Is It Time to Retire the Word 'Wife'"? (*The Huffington Post*, Feb. 15, 2012)

"Do You Hate Your Husband?" (*Yahoo!*, Dec. 5, 2010)

"Stay-at-home moms more depressed than working moms, study finds" (*Today Show*, May 18, 2012)

Headlines like these are commonplace. They are *the norm*. (And by the way, can you even imagine a headline that read, "Do You Hate Your Wife?" The double standard is shocking.) But if you'd been born in an earlier era, it would *never occur to you* to think along these lines. You wouldn't be resentful toward men, nor would you assume marriage is suffocating. Instead, the messages you'd receive from society, *despite your parents' example*, would be positive. Helpful. They would be pro-marriage and pro-family.

You just happen to have been born at a time when fractured families are the rule, not the exception. Almost everyone you know has either been divorced or has been affected by divorce. Moreover, your source of support and camaraderie is no longer family and community. It's media.

Strangers.

Women with whom you have nothing in common.

Which brings us to the million-dollar question: How are you going to block out this "terrible conspiracy of noise"?[15] Are you going to live intentionally? Or mindlessly?

As I see it, you have two options. You can absorb the messages and make decisions based on what the prevailing culture tells you is the 'thing to do' (and thus live an unexamined life). Or, you can tune out what you see and hear around you and go with your gut. Because if you regularly absorb pop culture—and by that I mean mainstream news media, television sitcoms and dramas, women's magazines, and Hollywood films—your views on men and marriage are being heavily influenced by all the wrong people.

Your friends will deny this vociferously. "Oh, I watch and read that stuff," they'll say, "but it doesn't affect me." I'm sure they believe that, but it's naïve.

Here's an idea: Try turning off mainstream television for a week and watch black-and-white films instead. Or better yet, read a romance novel from the early twentieth century. Afterward, see if the way you look at love isn't different. I'd be shocked if it isn't.

The folks who produce the material that gets delivered to your doorstep every day—via television, magazines, and the Internet— depend on your absorbing their messages. These folks are in business because women like you consume the material they create.

Lest you think I'm exaggerating, former editor of *Ladies' Home Journal* Myrna Blyth exposed these folks in *Spin Sisters*: "Spin sisters are members of the female media elite, a Girls' Club of editors, producers, and print and television journalists with similar attitudes and opinions who influence the way millions of American women think and feel about their lives, their world, and themselves."[16]

And what are the spin sisters selling? The absurd notion that American women are unduly burdened, that they have the cards stacked against them, and that they're ultimately better off without men.

In other words, modern women's views on men and marriage have been filtered through a feminist lens, rather than through the lens of everyday Americans who have your best interests at heart. The women in the media may know a lot about reading a teleprompter, but their personal lives are a mess. They're the last people on earth who should be dispensing advice about marriage and motherhood.

Now I wish I could say that's all there is to it. Unfortunately, even if you steer clear of pop culture, many of your friends will not—which means they'll have a different take than you will on how things should be. As a result, your friends may try to steer you in a direction you don't want to go. That's why trends are so powerful. Even if *you* reject them, they affect you indirectly via your friends. And rejecting your friends, or at least their advice and opinions, is significantly harder than rejecting the media.

To say trends are powerful isn't enough—they're wicked. We humans suffer constant turmoil over what we believe is the right thing to do versus what we know is the popular thing to do. It begins when we're young and never lets up; adults are just as bad as kids. I know plenty of adults who compare themselves to their neighbors incessantly, not necessarily because they want to be better but because they want to fit in. They want to belong, even at the expense of doing what's best for themselves and their families.

Don't let this be your fate. Stop caring right now, today, about what other people think and do—whether it's the women in the media or the woman next door. If you want to make choices commensurate with what *you* want as opposed to what other people say you should want, you have to do this.

Deep down, most women want to get married and have a family; they're just too afraid to admit it. They think the desire to be a wife and mother means being less than what a woman can, or should, be. As writer/producer Dani Klein Modisett admitted in an article entitled "My Kids Stole My Ambition!" being employed was how she "justified her existence."[17]

Ms. Modisett is not alone. Many, many women feel this way, and it makes perfect sense given the environment in which they were raised. You've been taught to value money and prestige over love and family.

Reject this message. Instead, listen to your gut. Live an examined life. "Your time is limited, so don't waste it living someone else's life," said the late Steve Jobs. "Don't be trapped by dogma—which is living with the results of other people's thinking. Don't let the noise of others' opinions drown out your own inner voice. Have the courage to follow your heart and intuition. They somehow already know what you truly want to become."[18]

GET OVER YOURSELF

Step #2 of your detox is an extension of Step #1, and it has to do with your friends. You know, the ones who told you you're crazy for even *thinking* about marriage until you've "found yourself."

The idea that people should "find themselves" before getting married has been around since I was your age and has become even more pronounced over the years. The idea is that you first become the person you're supposed to, or "meant to," become and only then should you entertain the idea of settling down.

It's a lovely notion, the idea of finding oneself. In fact, theoretically I like it. And I get the point: We all need to grow a bit before hitching ourselves to someone else.

It's not that I don't think women (or men, for that matter) should live on their own and figure out what they want before getting married—I absolutely do. It's the concept of "finding oneself" that disturbs me.

Very few people "find" themselves in their twenties or even thirties. It takes *decades* to figure out who we are and what we're capable of. I'm fifty-three and still figuring out! The late Julia Child felt the same way. "I was thirty-seven years old and still discovering who I was."[19]

This is what's known as the process of maturation, and it happens as a result of living a very long time and having many different experiences—the most significant of which is marriage. Because it is in marriage where we are truly forced to grow and change.

One of my favorite quotes that I keep close by is by preacher Chuck Swindoll, who said, "Life is 10 percent what happens to you and 90 percent how you react to it."[20] People's priorities change when they get married. When you're single, life outside of work is largely without obligations or sacrifice. When you're married with children, you learn the art of compromise and unconditional love. *That's* when you truly "find yourself."

A woman named Ariana Jalfen left a great comment online in an article about marriage. She said, "Growth hand-in-hand with a like-minded person is the point—not growth in order to meet a like-minded person. Unless the goal is to marry a mirror image of yourself (with a penis), there's no need to become the person you want to attract."

So, living on one's own before getting married is important, yes, but not because by the age of say, thirty, you'll have discovered who you are. It's important because you should learn how to be self-sufficient should the occasion arise.

This is a great tool. I would never suggest, for example, that a woman not get an education because she plans to devote her life to family. None of us can predict the way our lives will unfold—we should all be prepared for the unforeseen.

The problem with the "finding oneself" argument is that the years of living solo tend to drag on and become counterproductive to real growth. Somewhere along the line, the stated goal gets lost in the shuffle. "Whereas delaying marriage and avoiding commitment would seem to promote self-discovery, this freedom and self-exploration seems to leave many people feeling more lost than found," writes Barry Schwartz in *The Paradox of Choice*.[21]

Makes sense, doesn't it? It's not as though your single friends have embarked on some sort of spiritual meditation. They probably spend their days going to the office, hitting the bars, watching TV, and having sex. Many stay in school for upwards of a decade or longer, either bleeding their parents dry or racking up serious debt. They don't spend ten or fifteen years in some sort of perfect self-exploration and then say, "Okay, I'm ready to get married now!" as if the growth period is over and Mr. Right is sitting patiently on the sidelines. On the contrary, one of three things usually occurs:

1. The woman gets bored trying to find herself or realizes her clock is ticking, at which point she decides she'd better hurry up and get married. Only trouble is, she can't find a marriageable man.

2. The woman finds a man to marry but realizes sometime later that she chose him out of convenience and that he wasn't the right choice of husband after all.

3. The woman marries a perfectly good man but suffers a huge emotional and financial toll trying to conceive even one child, let alone two.

Rachel Lehmann-Haupt is one such woman. In an article entitled "The Aniston Syndrome," she wrote that just before her thirty-seventh (thirty-*seventh!*) birthday, she told the man she loved that she was ready to settle down and have a child. "I've had all this freedom to come this far in my career, and I've finally found myself, and as a result I found you," she told him. "Now I have no control over my biology."[22]

Turns out her guy didn't want to get married. And of her "waning fertility," he callously responded, "It's nature's cruel joke on women."[23]

Lehmann-Haupt has it all wrong. She didn't find the love of her life as a result of finding herself. She's simply repeating the script she was sold.

Like so many women of her generation, Lehmann-Haupt was focused exclusively on herself and her career and thought Mr. Right would magically appear according to her own timetable. She was then willing to settle for the man she happened to be with at the time. "If I could go back ten years," she says, "I would tell my younger self that she should deeply consider her future family . . . I wonder whether in fact my generation collectively screwed up."[24]

What women like Lehmann-Haupt learned the hard way is that delaying marriage indefinitely in order to find oneself really just translates to "pursuing advanced degrees, establishing oneself in the workforce, and living day to day." And that course of action, over too long a time, is counterproductive if the goal is to get married and settle down.

Now if marriage and motherhood are not your goal, fine. More power to you. Take Kathryn Kelly, who was featured in *The Wall Street Journal*. When Ms. Kelly was young, her goal was to become a chef. She ended up drifting from that goal and instead got multiple degrees in public health and worked for years in the corporate sector. After she tired of that, she decided to pursue her lifelong dream and enroll in culinary school.

Two years after graduation, Kelly was offered a job at Oceania Cruises as a chef. Today, she spends ten months at sea and "has to stop and pinch herself" every now and then when she realizes she's an actual chef who gets to lead onshore excursions to markets and restaurants in places like Sicily, where she learned to "make cannoli and tasted lava-grown wine on Mount Etna."[25]

Ms. Kelly's life sounds glamorous, doesn't it? Very cool, indeed. But in order for Kelly to live the life she's chosen, she had to forgo a traditional marriage and family life. (The story did mention a daughter Kelly "raised on her own" somewhere along the way, but no other details were given.) Few people can pursue this kind of life if they want to have a family. Something's got to give.

The concept of finding oneself originated around the time of the sexual revolution. By the time you and your friends were born, America had fully embraced the New Age philosophy that baby boomers set forth more than forty years ago. Prior to the 1960s, Americans hadn't heard of this notion. They were too busy dealing with the realities of life to engage in such an existential crisis. That was a boomer thing.

People also weren't focused on the self. Prior to the 1960s, Americans embraced a universal moral order. This was a philosophy that focused on the health and well-being of *everyone*, not just the needs and desires of the individual.

This moral order wasn't necessarily a religious order (though that was part of it); it was more of an understanding that as citizens of a large community, we have a moral obligation to do the right thing and take into account how our choices affect those around us. Americans, for the most part, agreed on right and wrong, believed in God, and viewed family as society's great stabilizer.

But several factions emerged in the 1960s—antiwar activists and the feminist movement, for example—to turn this moral order on its head. Rather than expecting people to obey God or to subscribe to a universal concept of right and wrong, these groups argued that people should focus on what's best for them as individuals. Before long, voilà, the idea of being "true to oneself" was born.

This New Age philosophy still exists today and has officially replaced the universal moral order to which Americans once adhered. Religion is no longer a unifying force. Rather, we are mired in moral relativism, or the freedom to do what we want, when we want, with no judgment or interference from society. To many people, moral relativism *is* a religion.

Referring to life in the '60s, Charles Murray wrote, "To accept the concept of virtue requires that you believe some ways of behaving are right and others are wrong always and everywhere. That openly judgmental stand is no longer acceptable in America's schools, nor in many American homes."[26]

That's because moral relativism wiped it out.

But this self-centered approach to life—doing what you want, when you want—rarely produces the desired result. Instead it fosters a life that becomes so self-serving that when women eventually do get married—if they can find a man who's willing to marry them—it becomes difficult, if not impossible, to shift gears and take into account other individuals who have needs and desires of their own.

Moral relativism is a stain on American culture, as it holds people back from their true potential as human beings—as individuals, as spouses, and as parents. Those who came of age in the last several decades have no frame of reference for thinking or acting selflessly. They've been taught that the needs of the individual should always take precedence.

The children of boomers—millennials—have it even worse: They've been taught to believe they're "special" and that they're somehow deserving just for arriving in the world. Did you hear the commencement speech from Dr. David McCullough of Wellesley High School, including his now infamous proclamation, "You're Not Special"? Google it.

McCullough's point is that this generation has been so "pampered, cosseted, doted upon . . . feted and fawned over and called sweetie pie" that they've lost the understanding—and benefit—of what it means to work hard, sacrifice, and commit" to something greater than themselves.

> *"You are not exceptional. Contrary to what your U9 soccer trophy suggests, your glowing seventh grade report card, despite every assurance of a certain corpulent purple dinosaur, that nice Mr. Rogers and your batty Aunt Sylvia, no matter how often your maternal caped crusader has swooped in to save you, you are nothing special . . .*

> *. . . The fulfilled life is a consequence, a gratifying byproduct. It's what happens when you're thinking about more important things. Climb the mountain not to plant your flag, but to embrace the challenge, enjoy the air and behold the view. Climb it so you can see the world, not so the world can see you. Go to Paris to be in Paris, not to cross it off your list and congratulate yourself for being worldly. Exercise free will and creative, independent thought not for the satisfactions they will bring you, but for the good they will do others, the rest of the 6.8 billion—and those who will follow them. And then you too will discover the great and curious truth of the human experience is that selflessness is the best thing you can do for yourself.*[27]

If you want to get married and have kids, selflessness is a pre-requisite. If you want to be successful in this realm, you need to ignore all that coddling you've been given and stop thinking in terms of what you think you deserve or are entitled to. To have a fulfilling, beautiful life—the best life you can have—you don't need to *find* yourself.

You need to get over yourself.

FIND YOUR FEMININE

You know those women who have it all together professionally but can't for the life of them get their love lives in order? There's actually a phrase for these ladies: "smart in life, dumb in love."

I read an article by a woman named Kris Fuchs who said, "My business runs just fine. It's my personal life I find so difficult."[28] For many women today, this is par for the course.

Highly educated, professional women used to be a rare breed, but today they're commonplace. But it's not a coincidence that at the same time women have "risen" in the marketplace, their marriages and relationships have taken a nosedive.

Power and love are hopelessly at odds. The same skills that will get you ahead in the marketplace—being aggressive or being a perfectionist, for example—are the exact skills that will destroy your love life.

To find love, you must develop and embrace your feminine gifts. If you can do this, you'll find a different kind of power awaits you.

This likely sounds foreign to you. You've been so focused on outward achievement, it will be hard to get in touch with your softer side. Women have suffocated their femininity in order to prove something to themselves and to the world. As singer/songwriter

Rachel Fine wrote in an article for The Huffington Post, "I've always thrived in a man's world, and to do that, you almost have to shut off your girlie side."

It isn't surprising that women feel they need to "shut off their girlie side." Since the day they were born, they've been encouraged to ignore their hardwiring. They've been conditioned to believe that women live in a culture in which the cards are stacked against them—and that to rectify this so-called problem, they must chuck their feminine proclivities and become more like men.

It is precisely this attitude that keeps lasting love at bay.

In order for love to thrive, there must be two energies at play: the masculine and the feminine. But femininity has vanished from American culture. Until women bring it back, love will continue to be elusive.

So what does it even mean to be feminine? I think a lot of women genuinely don't know what this means. Put simply, to be feminine is to be soft, nurturing, and receptive—as opposed to gruff and aggressive. That's male territory.

Being soft, nurturing, and receptive is not the same thing as being a mouse, by the way. Men love women who are fun and feisty and who know their own mind! But they don't want a fire-eating dragon. And they don't want a woman's strength to overpower theirs, not because they can't handle it (as you'll hear many women say) but because they don't want to handle it. They don't want another man to contend with; they do that all day. What they want when they're with you is peace. Fighting with women isn't in men's nature.

I know you've been taught to chuck your femininity, or your soft and nurturing ways, to become more like men: dominant, aggressive, and in charge. But you're paying a price. A woman's love, along with her femininity, can reduce the most powerful man in the world to mere jellyfish. Your husband, whether he's a CEO or a handyman, wants to make you happy more than anything else in the world. It's what he lives for.

The biological differences between women and men are real, and they are hardwired. Masculine energy conquers and cogitates. It likes to do things, and it likes to be alone to think about how to do those things.

Feminine energy nurtures and verbalizes. It likes to talk, and to be pampered and doted upon. That's why feminine energy is the receiver of masculine energy. It's why men typically make the first move in a relationship and why the man asks the woman for her hand in marriage, rather than the other way around. The male acts, and the female responds.

The fact that men are *capable* of nurturing and women are *capable* of conquering doesn't change the fact that this is typically not where each sex's natural energy flows. Men and women are as different as night and day, and these differences are a deeply rooted part of evolutionary biology.

"Male and female brains are different from the moment of conception," wrote neuropsychiatrist Louann Brizendine. "There are deep differences, at the level of every cell, between the male and female brain. A male cell has a Y chromosome and the female does not. That small but significant difference begins to play out early in the brain as genes set the stage for later amplification by hormones."[29]

As an example, Brizendine describes one of her patients who gave her toddler daughter a handful of unisex toys, including a bright red fire truck. "She walked into her daughter's room one afternoon to find her cuddling the truck in a baby blanket, rocking it back and forth saying, 'Don't worry, little truckie, everything will be all right.'"[30]

There's nothing unusual about this scenario—it's typical, everyday stuff. But women have become so far removed from their natural tendencies, they no longer recognize they have them.

When was the last time you saw a wife or girlfriend be kind and nurturing toward her husband or boyfriend? When was the last time you saw her let him hold the door open for her? Or pay the bill? Or look at him when he talks as though he has something important to say? These are old-fashioned feminine habits, and they work—in every era.

The other night I was on a date with my husband, and the woman next to us was berating her husband the entire time. Neither my husband nor I said anything until we got in the car. We were so horrified we decided they must be brother and sister because it was too painful to think their relationship was real. It was . . . ugly. That's the only word I can use to describe it.

Too many women today are "ugly." Mean. Hard. Women like this have been around for centuries, but it was never commonplace the way it is today.

There was a time, believe it or not, when men were respected members of society. They had a role to play, and it was an important one. Women *liked* men and sought them out. "Landing" a husband was considered a coup. Imagine!

Of course that was before women felt the need to prove they're just like men. And since men by nature tend to be rough, hard, and competitive—as opposed to soft and sweet—now women are, too.

"Feminism is central to the state of love today because it rejects the complementary character of men and women—an idea that is central to our cultural tradition. As different as we are, we need one another, and any theory that does not understand that pattern will be destructive," wrote Kenneth Minogue in *The Wall Street Journal*.[31]

And it has been. Modern orthodoxy suggests biology is adaptable, not determinative. You've been raised to believe one's gender shouldn't dictate one's choices. Men can do what women can do, and women can do what men can do.

Not only can they; deep down they want to. The only reason there aren't more female firefighters and more male preschool teachers is because parents and society raise the sexes to think a certain way—you know, by giving girls dolls and boys trucks, that sort of thing.

Feminists have been so successful preaching this myth (even though the most outspoken among them don't have children and thus have no idea what they're talking about) that your generation grew up thinking males and females have the same goals, desires, and abilities.

Should you run into any disparities in this regard—and you will—it's not due to biology, you're told. It simply proves we live in a patriarchy. The "patriarchy" is the reason women make less than men. It's the patriarchy's fault there aren't more female CEOs or more stay-at-home dads.

But this radical concept of gender is new. It may be all *you* know, but you're not that old. Most Americans didn't grow up with this mythical view of male and female nature. It has always been understood that men bring something to the table that women don't, and vice versa.

You've probably heard your friends talk about men in a disparaging manner. And yet, isn't it interesting they still want to get married? Sadly, they're going to struggle to find (and keep) a husband—for two reasons.

One, they have their dukes up. That's not a relationship; that's war. Two, they don't understand men and thus don't appreciate the male/female dance. *What it takes to get a man into bed is not the same as what it takes to get a man to the altar.* Your generation desperately needs an education on relationship dynamics.

So let's get started.

A long, long time ago, people didn't know why men and women were different, but intuition and common sense told them all they needed to know: Men and women are vastly different creatures. Unfortunately, your generation has been taught that equality means sameness, or interchangeability. Thus, in order to actually believe the sexes are different, you need proof.

Fortunately, we have it. The research on brain differences has exploded over the past decade—it's all there in black and white. For instance, did you know the female brain secretes more serotonin than the male brain? Serotonin is important because it relates directly to impulse control. Men are far more likely than women to drink and drive, for example. They're also more prone to suicide.

And sex? As we already learned, sex takes up a lot of space in the male brain. The best illustration I can offer about the difference between men and women when it comes to sex is this: How many men do you know who'd be offended if a woman told him she'd like to use his body for sex? Now turn that scenario around. If a man told a woman he'd like to use her body for sex, it would be grounds for sexual harassment. Apples and oranges.

And remember when we talked about oxytocin, the bonding hormone and neurotransmitter that keeps women from being able to have sex without strings attached? Oxytocin isn't just relevant when it comes to sex; it's also the reason little girls like to play with "care objects." It's why my daughter would find any inanimate object she could when she was little and pretend it was a baby so she could cradle it, rock it to sleep, and change its diaper.

On the other hand, that males have less serotonin—which again, regulates impulse control—than females is the reason my son would find any inanimate object when he was little and pretend it had the power to kill. I suspect their lower amounts of serotonin is also the reason males love to—Lord I hate this word—fart. If I had a dollar for every time my son used to purposefully fart as loud as he could, followed by fits of laughter, I'd be rich.

Parents don't *teach* their little girls to be caregivers, nor do they *teach* their little boys to be unruly, as society suggests. These desires are hardwired.

Females also have an accelerated occipital lobe. This allows their brains to take in more sensory data than boys—which, if you think about the way men and women communicate, makes perfect sense. Women love to analyze things to death, whereas men just want the final conclusion of all that rumination. How many times has a guy asked you to get to the point? Oy vey, I'm embarrassed to answer that one . . .

Finally, there's a part of the brain called the hippocampus. Its main job is memory storage, and it is much larger in females than it is in males. Michael Gurian wrote about this in his books *The Wonder of Girls* and *The Wonder of Boys*. He used an example of a young boy and a young girl being asked by their parents to do three things around the house: clean up their rooms, take out the garbage, and wipe the table. He said that more often than not, we will see the young girl complete the tasks with less reminding than the boy would need and that this has a lot to do with the hippocampal memory. Men are linear in their thinking. Generally speaking, they can focus only on one thing at a time.

Does this sound spurious? If so, that's because you've been conditioned to believe the reason women do more housework and child care is because their chauvinistic husbands expect them to—and that unless men start pulling their weight at home, women will never achieve equality. But most men don't *expect* women to do all the work at home. They just *don't care* whether or not the laundry gets done or the beds get made. My husband's idea of dusting is to wipe a surface clean with the sweep of his arm. Hello?

Now I'm not suggesting that because men don't care as much about these things, you should do everything yourself. I'm saying that recognizing your husband operates differently than you do will go a long way toward creating peace at home. There's a way to get a man to be more proactive at home, and expecting him to be like you isn't it.

That the sexes aren't "equal," as in the same, has no bearing on the value of each gender or on what each sex contributes to society as a whole. Your perception of equality is simply skewed.

Men and women are equal in value but wildly different by nature. They do not have the same bodies, they do not speak the same language, they're not motivated by the same things, and they do not operate with the same set of tools. Men are men, and women are women. It stands to reason, then, that acting as if male and female are one and the same hinders us rather than helps us.

But make any reference to the differences between the sexes and the media go ballistic. They'll tell you people like me are throwbacks who think the sexes each have their "place," and we should therefore adhere to strict gender roles.

Perhaps some people believe that, but I'm not one of them. And quite frankly, I don't know anyone who is.

Every couple I know has some crossover with respect to gender roles, myself included. But that doesn't mean we reject the fact that men and women are different, or that we think society's to blame for these differences. Nor does it mean we think men and women should be equally represented in all spheres of life in order to prove some false notion of equality. That's ridiculous.

The best example of male and female nature I've seen was depicted in *My Big Fat Greek Wedding*. Did you see it? The daughter, Toula, is upset because she can't get her very traditional Greek father to understand that she wants more out of life than just being a wife, so her mother steps in to teach her daughter how women use certain strategies when dealing with men. "Let me tell you something, Toula. The man is the head [of the household], but the woman is the neck. And she can turn the head any way she wants."[32]

Modern women have no appreciation for the power wives yield on the home front. The average husband *wants* to please his wife. He wants her to be happy and will do anything in his power to make it happen. "To us," wrote comedian Steve Harvey in *Act Like a Lady, Think Like a Man*, "your power comes from one simple thing: you're a woman, and we men will do anything humanly possible to impress you so we can be with you. You're the ultimate prize for us."[33]

Meanwhile, all men want in exchange is respect, kindness, and sex. There isn't much more to it than that.

Unfortunately, these things have all taken a backseat in marriage. Modern American women have been taught to be mistrustful of and disrespectful toward men. If you have any doubt about this, just turn on any sitcom and it'll be clear as day. Women talk to and about men as if they're idiots. I've personally witnessed wives (you probably have to) who roll their eyes at their husbands' comments, mock their husbands' salaries, or freely admit to not sleeping with them.

These women may as well put a dagger in their husbands' hearts and twist it around and around.

The saddest part is, these women genuinely don't realize they're destroying their marriages. Why would they? Their behavior is not only encouraged, it's mirrored by the women they see around them. They have no reason to think they're doing anything wrong.

I'm convinced our grandmothers would be shocked if they knew the extent of what goes on in marriages today. But of course our grandmothers were never saddled with such high expectations of marriage, plus they respected men and accepted the reality of men's sex drive. Just imagine if we still did!

Unfortunately, women today think of marriage solely as a romantic venture, so *duty* and *obligation* are unfamiliar terms. In fact, the idea of being morally (and even legally) required to have sex with one's spouse sounds nuts. Many wives joke that their husbands should be grateful for anything they get.

But spouses *do* have a duty to sleep with one another. Sex is the glue that holds a marriage together.

To get inside the mind of a man, I decided to ask Sam, a celebrity interviewer in Los Angeles, to explain what men want. Sam is forty-two and divorced (no kids), and he has a super body he works hard to maintain. Having joined eHarmony years ago, he has read thousands of profiles and has had countless first dates. He seems to have a good handle on what women want but says women don't understand what men need. Here's what he told me:

> *Sex is a man's only emotional connection—it's like a woman's desire for communication. Men don't like to communicate through lengthy discussions; that's why they always ask women to get to the point.*
>
> *A woman's primary M.O.—communication—is rarely pleasurable for men. Yet a man's primary M.O.—sex—is very pleasurable for women. So when a man asks his wife for sex, he's not asking her*

to do something that's not pleasurable, or something that only benefits him. He loves bringing pleasure to his wife. It's how he communicates his love for her.

You can't turn this around. Oftentimes a man likes to have no communication at all—yet if he doesn't spend hours listening to his wife or girlfriend talk about her feelings or problems, he's considered a prick. Why, then, should women be allowed to say no to sex whenever it suits them? That would be like a man cutting off all communication with his wife or girlfriend when it doesn't suit him. It would be like a husband saying this to his wife: "Listen, honey, in marriage sometimes things happen—people close to us become ill, or die, or one of us gets depressed, etc.—so I think it's reasonable when I don't feel like talking, listening, or paying any attention to you. I just don't feel like communicating. Thanks for under-standing—just like you expect me to understand the no-sex thing."[34]

Sam also added that most of the profiles he receives are from women who present themselves as powerful and independent, as though these are salable traits. But men aren't impressed with that. What men want more than anything else in the world is to be respected and admired, loved and accepted. The rest is immaterial.

Sam's comments about sex are eerily similar to those of Steve Harvey, who referred to sex as "the cookie" in *Act Like a Lady.* "Please—puh-leeze—don't hold out on the cookie," he wrote. "We don't care about anything else; we need the cookie. The emotional stuff—the talking, the cuddling, the holding hands, and bonding, that's y'all's thing. We'll do those things because we know it's important to you. But please understand: the way we men connect is by having sex. Period."[35]

These differences we're talking about between men and women start early, by the way. They're visible at birth and become even more pronounced in grade school. As a former teacher and the mother of a boy and a girl, I can personally attest to boys' need to move their bodies or just *do something* active, and girls' preference for sedentary activities that require being verbal.

As a small example, some months ago my daughter had four friends sleep over for her birthday. What did they do? Talked. The entire time. For hours. And the next morning they played "Truth or Dare?" How many boys do you know who (a) have sleepovers, (b) talk all night, and (c) play "Truth or Dare?" in the morning? Honestly, I could fill an entire book with examples of differences between males and females.

What women need to understand is that the *faux version of equality they've been taught undermines love.*

Men are hunters. They want to build things and kill things—that's why more men than women use guns. It's why male engineers greatly outnumber female engineers. Women, on the other hand, like to gather and nest—that's why more women than men like to go shopping or go to lunch, or stay home with their kids. Women also like to get all dressed up and prance about in their heels. And men love to watch women prance about in their heels.

That's the yin and yang of gender relations.

Unfortunately, modern women have lost sight of this fact, or perhaps never understood it in the first place. They were told power comes from being masculine, or thinking and behaving like a man. This may have resulted in women becoming rich and successful, but they have lost their power in love.

A woman's real power lies in her femininity, not in her ability to emulate or compete with men. Remember when I said that what it takes to get a man into bed is not the same as what it takes to get a man to the altar? Harvey explained this concept in a chapter titled "Sports Fish vs. Keepers."

Men, he wrote, fish for women. But they can only catch what they're able to reel in. "Men will treat women like one of two things: a sports fish or a keeper. A sports fish doesn't have any rules, requirements, respect for herself, or guidelines; and we men can pick up her scent a mile away. She's the party girl." He added, "As soon as she lets a man know he can treat her just any old kind of way, he will do just that."

A keeper, on the other hand, "never gives in easily," he continued. Her high standards and expectations are evident from the get-go. A keeper "understands her power and wields it like a samurai sword. She commands—not demands—respect, just by the way she carries herself."

And here's my favorite part because it's *so* true: "Men automatically know *from the moment she opens her mouth* [emphasis mine] that if they want her, they'll have to get in line with her standards and requirements."[36]

This psychological seesaw, which has been played out between men and women for centuries, has been eradicated by a society that pushes a unisex agenda. Women have no idea how to use their femininity to their advantage, so they end up rearing their heads, trying to be something they're not. They become competitors of men.

It's the biggest mistake women ever made.

A woman's femininity is unbelievably powerful. It doesn't lower a woman's status, nor does it preclude her from being her own person. Men love a woman who knows her own mind! So, go. Do what you want with your life—no one's stopping you. Just don't try to compete with your husband.

Men don't want a competitor at home; they have plenty of those at work. At the end of the day, what a man wants is a woman who's soft and nurturing and kind—and who's just as concerned with his needs as she is with her own, maybe even more. That's what it means to love.

Let human nature do its thing. Men like to chase women, and women like to be chased—that's just the way it is. Don't become the hunter. Don't call a guy or make the first move. Don't try to take charge or be in control. That's what men are supposed to do. So let them.

If you can manage to tap into your femininity without feeling victimized, you will find the love you so desperately seek. Our post-feminist culture is fighting a gender war that I can assure you has no winner.

My advice is to stay out of it.

DON'T RELY ON LOVE ALONE

I'm sure you know this already, at least theoretically, but I must be-labor it. Everything that comes out of Hollywood, from conception to delivery, is an illusion. A fabrication. False. Fake. A *lie*.

Hollywood is one giant temptation to get you to screw up your life in every conceivable way.

That's why I spent so much time in Step #1 trying to explain the necessity of rejecting pop culture. Because that's what Holly-wood is: pop culture. It doesn't matter whether we're talking about movies, television, or even the music you listen to. It all emanates from the same place, and almost all of it is toxic.

Now if you're *not* looking for lasting love, by all means zone out in fairy tale land. Have a party. But if you're looking for a *real* life with a *real* man, you're going to have to reject Hollywood.

Hollywood needs you to believe in fairy tales. It depends on your absorbing its messages and coming back for more. Women inhale "rom-coms" and music with lyrics about love because they desperately want to believe in happily ever after. But happily-ev-er-after doesn't exist.

I don't mean there's no happy ending in the real world. I mean the *image* you have of happily ever after does not in any way, shape, or form match the reality. The real happily-ever-after is 100 percent different from what you imagine. The girl and the guy don't walk off into the sunset together.

Well, they do—but the sun will set on some very hard times. Hollywood skips over that part.

It is simply impossible to overstate the impact television has had on your life. Television has literally altered the human mind and contributed to the breakdown of marriage and families, thanks to the lies it sells to women, in particular, about what relationships should look like. The idea that love is all you need abounds in just about every story you absorb.

But to have a marriage that lasts—and please read this over and over again because I literally can't emphasize it enough—*you cannot rely on love alone.* Two people who intend to be married for a lifetime need much more than love to keep them going. Much more.

A great illustration of how screwed up our priorities are is how engaged women spend all their time focused on their wedding day and virtually no time focusing on the marriage itself.

They have it all backwards. Weddings are irrelevant in the grand scheme of things. Except for the vows, it's all fluff. After the wedding and honeymoon are over and several years have passed, life settles in—and if a couple got married mainly because they had warm and gooey feelings for each other, or because they couldn't envision a life without the other person, that marriage is doomed.

I know when you're in love it's hard *not* to think of your guy as your very own Prince Charming who's going to make you eternally happy, but, at some point, reality is going to smack you in the face.

For one thing, it's not your husband's job to make you happy. For another, *no one person can possibly fulfill all your deepest desires.* That's too much to put on one person. It sets up an impossible situation, for him and for you.

To be honest, there are going to be moments as a wife when you'll doubt your choice. Perhaps you'll see some sharp-jawed, blue-eyed male specimen picking out tomatoes in aisle 6 of your local grocery store and wonder if you made a mistake, or if you could have done better. Hollywood tells you these vulnerabilities indicate your relationship is on the rocks. It tells you no one in the *right* relationship ever doubts his or her decision. It tells you love comes in the shape of a six-pack and a sultry week in Cape Cod.

But Hollywood only lasts two hours in the theater with a bag of overly buttered popcorn. Marriage lasts a lifetime. Or it's supposed to.

Believe it or not, the folks who ran Hollywood used to take their influence seriously. They used to produce films that were ethical and realistic, particularly when the theme was love. Take *Gone with the Wind*. In this film, the main character, Scarlett, is in love with Ashley. (Ashley is a man.) Ashley loves Scarlett, too; but he's engaged to Melanie.

Scarlett knows Ashley's engaged to Melanie, but Scarlett has no scruples, so she throws herself at Ashley every chance she gets. And while he's hopelessly drawn to Scarlett, Ashley refuses her advances and insists he's better suited to Melanie—even though Melanie doesn't light his fire the way Scarlett does. Here's the exchange between them:

Ashley: I'm going to marry Melanie.

Scarlett: But you can't, not if you care for me!

Ashley: Oh my dear, why must you make me say things that will hurt you? How can I make you un-

derstand? You're so young and unthinking, you don't know what marriage means.

Scarlett: I know I love you and I want to be your wife! You don't love Melanie!

Ashley: She's like me, Scarlett. She's part of my blood. We understand each other.

Scarlett: But you love me!

Ashley: How could I help loving you? You have all the passion for life that I lack. But that kind of love isn't enough to make a successful marriage for two people who are as different as we are.[37]

In 1939, Hollywood was literally bound by contract to impart moral messages and avoid subjects that were considered improper. If *Gone with the Wind* had been made today, with the universal moral order no longer in place, Ashley and Scarlett would be involved in a torrid affair—before and after Ashley's marriage to Melanie.

I often wonder how many more successful marriages we'd have if people were exposed to films with messages that applied to real life, rather than being fed a diet of modern-day "rom-coms." As I wrote in Step #1, the kind of support and camaraderie we experience in our lives significantly affects, for better or for worse, the decisions we make.

It's not a coincidence the divorce rate was lower at a time when Hollywood produced films with strong moral messages.

Today, there's a whole new message coming out of Hollywood. "Hollywood says you can be deeply in love with someone and then your marriage will work. But you can be deeply in love with someone to whom you cannot be successfully married," wrote Father Pat Connor.[38]

Father Connor is a seventy-nine-year-old priest and counselor from Australia who speaks to high school seniors, mostly girls, about "whom not to marry." One of the things he tells them is that in most cases, infatuation trumps judgment.

If you're hesitant to take advice about marriage from a priest, you may find it interesting that Connor's message mirrors Dr. M. Scott Peck's. Now deceased, Dr. Peck authored the bestselling book, first published in 1978, called *The Road Less Traveled*. It stayed on *The New York Times* bestseller list for years. I was in college, in the mid-to-late '80s, when I first read it. What I remember most about it is the section on love. Specifically, the section on real love versus "falling in love."

"Of all the misconceptions about love," wrote Peck, "one of the most powerful and pervasive is the belief that 'falling in love' is love." There are two problems with this view, he said. The first is that the experience of falling in love is a "sex-linked erotic experience." The second is that it's "invariably temporary."[39]

No matter whom we fall in love with, Peck continued, "we sooner or later fall out of love if the relationship continues long enough ... The feeling of ecstatic lovingness that characterizes love always passes. The honeymoon always ends. The bloom of romance always fades."[40]

That was Ashley's point in *Gone with the Wind*: He knew the chemistry between Scarlett and him would fade, and they'd have nothing left to sustain them.

That our initial chemistry with a person ends sounds depressing, I know. That's not the way most of us probably wish it were. It must be even harder for someone in your generation to accept since you've been raised in a disposable world. Everything you desire is just a click away—and when you no longer want it, you just throw it out and find something else.

What this means for many people is that the moment their relationship hits a snag, the appeal of someone new—the desire for that "first kiss tingle" I heard Ryan Seacrest refer to once—can be overwhelming. But if you give in to it, you're buying yourself a boatload of trouble because you will never be satisfied. The same thing will happen over and over again with each new relationship. I have a friend who has been chasing it for decades. She's now twice divorced and alone, still looking for love.

Don't make the mistake so many people do. Don't assume that because the "feeling of ecstatic lovingness" ends, you've resigned yourself to boring sex or a dead love life. Relationships are designed to move on to the next phase. Your desire for your husband isn't going to end; it'll just take on a different feel. No two people can sustain that initial level of excitement for decades—it's impossible. So just know that going in.

Once you accept that "falling in love" is not love, that it's merely step one of what has the potential to become real love, your perspective on marriage will change dramatically. As Peck wrote in the opening paragraphs of his book, "Once we know that life is difficult—once we truly understand and accept it—then life is no longer difficult. Because once it is accepted, the fact that life is difficult no longer matters."[41]

Whether we're talking about life being difficult or the fact that "falling in love" isn't real love, the answer lies in *the decision to accept what is rather than hold on to a false version of what you want it to be.*

If you do, then down the road, when you've been married awhile, you don't freak out. You don't assume your marriage is doomed because you've lost that "first kiss tingle."

That's one of the reasons so many Hollywood marriages fail. When the feelings of ecstasy reach their expiration date, as they always do, people assume the marriage is over. That's because they built their lives on a fantasy.

I did that once—built my life on a fantasy. Only in my case it wasn't the "first kiss tingle" that consumed me; it was the idea that love conquered all.

I loved my first husband deeply. We weren't right for each other for a thousand different reasons, but I honestly believed I could love him so well our conflicts would be resolved. How ridiculous! How presumptuous! How stupid.

But I know I'm not alone. Countless women have made the same mistake. We learned the hard way that love, in fact, does not conquer all.

The truth is, my antenna went up on countless occasions during the course of my relationship with my ex—especially when the subject of children, religion, or politics came up. Unfortunately, it took starting a life together for the two of us to accept that he and I had entirely different values.

The things that were important to him weren't important to me, and vice versa. The things I believed in he didn't believe in, and vice versa. The way he handled problems and unforeseen conflicts was not the way I handled them. But in my romantic head, up until the last possible moment, I thought love was enough to see us through.

Please read this carefully: You can never love a man so hard and so well that your concerns will magically disappear, and you won't be the one woman who will prove it can be done. There was no lack of love between my ex and me. That's the one thing, maybe the only thing, we did have.

Bottom line: If you don't love a man *exactly as he is*, even if he never changes a stinkin' thing, get out. Father Connor addressed this point in his speech to young women. Here's some of what he said, paraphrased:

- Don't marry a problem character thinking you'll change him—for example, if he's a heavy drinker, don't think that if he just marries a good woman, he'll settle down. People are the same after marriage as before, only more so.

- Never marry a man who has no friends.

- Examine his nature. Does he possess those character traits that add up to a good human being? Conversely, do you see "red flag" behaviors? For example, is he inclined to fits of rage? If so, is he capable of admitting his faults and apologizing? If warning flags are waving in the wind, stay away!

- Take a good, unsentimental look at his family. Are his parents married or divorced? If your guy is a product of divorce, that may—indeed, probably will—bring with it a whole host of issues. If his parents are married, what is their marriage like? Does your guy have a good relationship with his parents?

There are so many things that aren't obvious when you're in love. In its early stages, love really is blind. But none of the points above should be ignored, particularly the part about your boyfriend's family of origin.

I suspect most people have "issues" of one sort or another with their parents, but what really matters are the messages about life and love that get passed on from parents to children. Ask yourself whether you agree with and respect the narratives your boyfriend's parents passed on to him.

The third point Father Connor made, to "examine his nature," is also critical. You need to be aware of how your boyfriend or fiancé reacts to things. Is he easily bothered or quick to anger? Is he compassionate and loving toward other people—not just you? Does he tend to be self-absorbed? Watch how he handles people: his co-workers, his boss, his nieces and nephews, even strangers. That should tell you a lot.

Over the course of my relationship with my ex there were many red flags, but I lacked the courage to face them. We were the opposite of those characters in the old movies, the ones who conceded the conflicts were too great to resolve and moved on.

Sometimes when you get so deep in a relationship, it's hard to believe life exists outside that person or that there could be someone else out there who's better suited for you. Or sometimes, let's face it: you just don't *want* to let him (or her) go. You love him and you want to be with him, and that's all there is to it.

So instead of facing the music, my ex and I focused on the good stuff. My ex was, at heart, a good man: He was loyal, he never cheated or lied, and he was affectionate and open with his feelings. He was very good to me for a long time, and he loved me *despite* my flaws. I was smitten. But in the end, it came down to two different people from two different worlds who wanted two very different lives.

Step #4 is simple to understand but hard to accept: When choosing a spouse, *you cannot rely on love alone*. If you fall in love with a man whose values and priorities differ sharply from yours, you will waste valuable time and energy, and invite a boatload of heartache to boot, trying to make the relationship into something it's not. You either share the same values and goals, or you don't.

Just forget about romantic love when it comes to choosing a spouse. Romance may be the path to a fun or even satisfying dating relationship—and it can certainly be the *start* of something potentially lasting—but it has nothing to do with sustaining a marriage.

Keep your feelings in perspective. You may love someone deeply, but that alone is no reason to marry him.

GET A RING, NOT A ROOMMATE

There was a time, believe it or not, when living with a boyfriend or girlfriend—"shacking up," it was called then—would have been an outlandish idea. It still should be viewed that way, in my opinion, but not for the reasons you might think.

Unfortunately, cohabitation has become so commonplace—it has increased in the United States over the past half century by more than 1,500 percent[42]—that it appears benign. But it isn't. As a marriage coach, I can tell you that almost every couple who reaches out to me in crisis was at one point "shacking up."

Just because something's popular doesn't mean it's harmless. That was the point of Step #1. In order to make good decisions, you must be able to step away from the prevailing culture and think for yourself. You need to ask yourself, "Is this smart? Does this feel right *in my gut*? Will this get me where I want to go?"

There are two main reasons people live together. Convenience is the most obvious. Since couples are sleeping over at each other's apartments every night anyway, they figure they can save a lot of time and money if they rent one apartment. The second reason couples move in together is to "test" the relationship, or to determine whether or not they're compatible.

But living with someone does not offer a couple the assurances they're looking for. In fact, it will work against your being successfully married.

The best research to date on this subject can be found in the ongoing study called the National Marriage Project. A nonpartisan, nonsectarian, and interdisciplinary initiative, the NMP was founded in 1997 by Drs. Popenoe and Barbara Dafoe Whitehead. Its mission is to provide research and analysis on the health of marriage in America, to analyze the social and cultural forces shaping contemporary marriage, and to identify strategies to increase marital quality and stability.

One of its findings is that living together before marriage—*unless the couple was engaged beforehand*—increases the risk of divorce. "The longer you live together with a partner," wrote Popenoe, "the more likely it is that the low-commitment ethic of cohabitation will take hold."[43] In other words, people who are used to living together never acquire the tools they need to stay the course because they always have an out. Their commitment to the relationship is therefore more fragile.

And commitment is really the issue. Cohabitation is simply commitment with an escape hatch—which, by that very definition, means it's not a commitment. It's also something people tend to fall into. A marriage, on the other hand, is a *decision* people make. Those are two very different things.

So what's the real reason men and women choose to cohabitate? What's the goal? Research shows women are more likely to view cohabitation as a step toward marriage, while men are likelier to see it as a way to postpone commitment. "This gender asymmetry is associated with negative interactions and lower levels of commitment even after the relationship progresses to marriage," wrote Meg Jay in *The New York Times*.[44]

Research aside, there are two main reasons you should not live with a man to whom you are not engaged. First, it doesn't allow for the objectivity you'll need in trying to determine whether or not he's "the one." The reason the statistics make an exception for couples who were engaged before they moved in together is because the weight of the decision about whom to marry rests on the day the choice is made. Most cohabitating couples haven't made any decision at all. They're just playing house.

But if you've already made the decision about whom to marry, moving in together before the wedding isn't all that significant to the health of the marriage. If you *haven't* made up your mind, if you're still deciding whether or not he's the one, living with him isn't going to help you make up your mind. On the contrary, it will cloud your judgment. You'll just get in deeper and deeper until eventually you can't see the forest through the trees. Living in separate spaces makes it much easier to make an informed decision.

Take Anna, for instance, who said she lived with her ex-husband before they got married and felt she was auditioning to be his wife. "We shared everything: furniture, bank accounts, animals, etc. By the time we hit our thirties, the next logical step was to get married." The decision to get married in situations like Anna's is haphazard; it just happens. It is not purposeful, the way getting engaged is supposed to be.

Getting married once you've already been living together becomes a default mechanism—because it seems like the next step, because someone wants a baby, because you're already doing it and, what the hell? Why not?—will almost always result in an unhappy ending. In such circumstances, marriage becomes a crapshoot rather than a commitment. A commitment is a purposeful decision made. The other is happenstance.

The second reason you should not live with someone to whom you're not engaged is because there's a psychological process that takes place once a decision is made. The way two people approach a marriage in which they assume they'll be together until "death do us part" is very different from a relationship in which the end is unknown.

"The very option of being allowed to change our minds," wrote Barry Schwartz, "seems to increase the chances we *will* change our minds. When we can change our minds about decisions, we are less satisfied with them. When a decision is final, we engage in a variety of psychological processes that enhance our feelings about the choice we made relative to the alternatives."[45]

This is one of the reasons, perhaps the main reason, so many cohabitating partners don't make it to the altar.

The decision about whom to marry has rarely been so tenuous. It used to be common, for example, for young people to seek their parents' advice and approval before becoming engaged. This may seem archaic to us, but it was sound practice. Parents can generally see what their grown children cannot since they're not emotionally invested in the relationship. Unfortunately, this practice went the way of the dinosaur. Being products of the divorce generation, young people can't rely on their parents' good advice. Their *grand-parents'*, perhaps. But not their parents'.

There's also this: While women today pretend to be fine with shacking up, I don't buy it. Lack of commitment makes most women uneasy. Remember: a woman's desire to bond is more pronounced than a man's. So no matter how content a woman may appear to be in a cohabitating relationship, deep down what she really wants is a ring. She wants a commitment. She wants to know she has someone there every night. Permanently.

A man's incentive to marry is different. Remember: Men are hunters. They want love, too; but the longer they can postpone commitment, the longer many of them will. Ultimately, a man's desire to marry stems from his "need to choose a particular woman and stay by her and provide for her if he is to know his children and they are to love him and call him father," wrote George Gilder in *Men and Marriage*. "Marriage asks men to give up their essential sexuality only as part of a clear scheme for replacing it with new, far more important roles: husband and father."[46]

That's not to say there aren't cohabitating couples where the man wants to get married and the woman doesn't. But regardless of who's holding back, the reason is essentially the same: fear of divorce, or fear that you're settling for less. Or both.

Also keep in mind that women, in particular, have been taught to believe they're entitled to perfection. So when they get a partner with flaws, which is the only kind to get, they begin to question the entire relationship.

Your story can be different. All you have to do is reject the idea that living with your guy is harmless. It is not "a step up" in your relationship; it's a step back.

If lasting love is the goal, get a ring—not a roommate.

MARRY THE ACCOUNTANT, NOT THE ARTIST

In her book *Marry Him*, author and psychotherapist Lori Gottleib wrote that she woke up one day to find herself unhappily single at the age of forty. In her analysis as to how it happened, she said that when she was in her twenties, her mother told her to stop going out with all those artist boyfriends she liked so much. She told Lori to find herself a man with a steady job, maybe one of those guys she thought was nerdy at one time but who turned out well on all fronts. Gottleib thought that was a bunch of old-fashioned drivel.

Then she wrote how stupid she was to reject her mother's advice.

That's how I came to title Step #6, "Marry the Accountant, Not the Artist." You can substitute *artist* with any career that doesn't provide a steady income and *accountant* with any career that does. The point isn't to focus on what your man does but on whether or not he's gainfully employed—or if he's a student, then at least on a clear path to becoming gainfully employed—before you consider marrying him.

That women aren't doing this today, that they are marrying men who lack purpose and direction—as well as steady, safe employment—is a massive problem that was virtually unheard of several generations ago.

Until recently, just about everyone understood that marriage-minded women need to marry men who can support them and their future children. It was accepted that women become vulnerable when they get pregnant and *at some point* will need a man on whom they can depend financially, if only for a few years. Without that, a woman has no options. She will not be able to take care of her baby when the time comes, no matter how badly she wants to.

People also understood, once upon a time, that babies need their mothers. Neither of these things—the vulnerability of pregnant women and the fact that mothers and babies belong together—has changed. Nor will they ever change.

What changed is the narrative. Rather than encourage women to expand their horizons outside of marriage and motherhood, as birth control and technological advances began to lighten the load on the home front, women were groomed to reject the needs of children altogether, to be suspect of men and marriage, and to become entirely self-sufficient.

It was terrible advice that has led to disastrous results.

As a marriage and relationship coach, I hear every week from the women who listened to and followed this narrative; and each of their stories has the same underlying component: Trained to overlook a man's earning potential and to become their own providers instead, women are now out-earning their husbands and boyfriends. They've become the breadwinners in the relationship—and they're miserable.

This is an entirely new set of circumstances your generation must contend with, similar to the negative effects of social media. My generation and all the ones preceding had none of this, and it is no small thing. Both are tearing relationships apart.

As a rule, wives who out-earn their husbands are not emboldened in this role the way men are. Rather, they become stressed out and resentful. Even young women who aren't married feel a sense of unease about moving forward in their relationship with this role reversal in place.

The mess that these women are now in is a direct result of the narrative they were sold about life and love. It was a massive sin of omission to remain silent about the fact that women's priorities change dramatically over time. What they thought was important when they were twenty-two will have significantly less value when they're thirty-two.

Most marriage-minded women do not want to be lifelong earners. Once they get close to the age of thirty, thoughts of marriage and motherhood begin to loom large. Indeed, baby fever is real—and almost every woman feels it. To pretend this is not the case and to steer women toward the workforce in the same way we steer men, as though the fact that women have babies and men do not doesn't change the entire conversation, is both irrational and nonsensical.

If you're a marriage-minded woman, and since you're reading this book I will assume you are, *you need to marry a man who can bring home the bacon.* He doesn't need to be rich, but he needs to make enough—or to be capable of making enough—to keep the family afloat.

As usual, this goes against everything you've been taught to believe. In fact, if some of your friends read this, they'd be shocked and even offended. "How retro! Who thinks that way anymore? What a loon." Well, they're certainly entitled to their opinion.

Even though it's wrong.

The reason parents have always taught their daughters to look for a man who can support them is because they knew that at some point their daughters would be home with their children and would therefore need a husband who made enough money to support a family.

None of this has changed just because there are more women in the workforce. Women are still the sex that gets pregnant, and they're still going to need a man on whom they can depend financially at some point, *even it's just for a few years*. At the very least, she will want options—whether it's 1955 or 2021.

In the past, both women *and men* prepared for the day when babies would arrive. Today, they do not. Since women are taught to pursue careers with the same verve as men, couples assume they'll both be in the workforce their entire lives—year-round and full-time. As a result, women make no preparations for motherhood and thus don't search for husbands who can support them. "We can take care of ourselves!" they insist.

That's the dumbest approach to life I've ever heard.

Liberated or not, the vast majority of women choose to quit their jobs or cut back when they have children. For some, it happens right away. For others, it takes the birth of a second or third child. Regardless, most women *do not stay in the workforce the way men do*: full-time, year-round, year after year after year.

Naturally, this puts today's woman in a precarious position since she has made plans for a completely different kind life.

Take Laurie Tennant, whose life as a working mother seemed to be working out fine: "I felt perfectly balanced," she said. It wasn't until her second child came, when Tennant was home on another maternity leave, that she had the opportunity to spend a considerable amount of time with her first child, who was by then several years older. Tennant was "jolted by how much she enjoyed the experience."[47] Shortly thereafter, she quit her job.

The single greatest mistake women make is mapping out their lives according to big career plans and paying no attention to how those plans will affect their lives down the line, when they become mothers. Women should do the exact opposite: Put marriage and motherhood, not career, at the center of your life—and fit everything else in around that.

Because the reality is, if you plan to be physically and emotionally present in your children's lives, you're going to need a husband on whom you can depend financially. This arrangement is neither foolish nor backward. It's just smart.

When women become mothers, they change—both emotionally and physiologically. What separates the women who choose to stay home from those who do not is that the first group ignored social trends and went with their gut. They planned to do so from the get-go and made decisions accordingly.

Most mothers do not remain permanently out of the workforce, but some do. My mother stayed home permanently with my sister and me after spending fifteen years as a stockbroker. My friend Lila has seven children, so that decision speaks for itself. But most mothers who stay home do so not because they don't ever plan to be employed again but because they want to *be* mothers, not just have children.

Other women make the decision to stay home when they realize daycare isn't cost-effective. A mother would have to make serious money to offset the costs incurred by living a dual-income lifestyle, at least when she has babies and toddlers at home. Unless she makes a six-figure salary, the money from a second income is usually eaten up by commuting costs, child care, eating out, work attire, dry cleaning, convenience foods, and, of course, taxes. By the time you add it up, there isn't much left.

And it's not just the money. These mothers incur an even greater loss because of the new lifestyle they've created: the loss of time. I have a friend Jane who lost her job as a sales rep for a pharmaceutical company when her daughters were five and nine. One of the main things she noticed about her new life is that she wasn't always rushing off somewhere. All of a sudden the world opened up to her. She had *time*.

The reason didn't flinch about the loss of income was because she and her husband didn't make financial decisions based on the assumption they'd always have two incomes.

That's what you should do, too.

The desire to have a life outside of work, children or no children, has been the subject of media attention as of late. A recent article in *The Wall Street Journal* highlighted women who are officially fed up with their all-consuming lifestyle of work, work, work. These women make big bucks, but they want their lives back. They want time to take a bike ride, to have coffee with friends, to cook, to exercise, and to travel for pleasure instead of for work.

Which goes back to my point about depending on a man. If you want a balanced life, you're going to *have* to depend on a man's more linear career goals—yet another difference between the sexes!—which are at the core of who men are as providers and protectors.

"Men are driven by who they are, what they do, and how much they make. No matter if a man is a CEO, a CON, or both, everything he does is filtered through his title (who he is), how he gets that title (what he does), and the reward he gets for the effort (how much he makes). These three things make up the basic DNA of manhood," wrote Steve Harvey.[48]

Now please don't start tallying up all the guys you know who don't fall into this category—there are always exceptions. But generally speaking, men don't feel good about themselves if they're not on a clear career path that allows them to support a family.

Problem is, women are now competing for this same role. And since most couples today assume women will remain in the workforce their entire lives, they make decisions according to that assumption. This impractical approach to life and love causes enormous conflict once couples become parents and see for themselves what's involved in raising children and maintaining a home.

The two-income lifestyle may be a win-win when children aren't in the picture—there's even a name for that: DINK (dual income, no kids)—but throw kids into the equation, and it's a whole different ballgame.

Just *imagine* how much more smoothly life would go if women assumed ahead of time that for x number of years they will need, and want, to depend on their husband's salary. If their assumptions about their lives are reversed—if women assume they *will* be home at some point, not that they won't—they can map out their lives accordingly.

This does *not* mean women need to marry rich men, just a stable one. In fact, if you do marry a rich man, or a man who's on that path, you will likely wind up feeling like a single mom since your husband will rarely be home. Rich men aren't home much, and you can't marry a man with that goal in mind and then complain later that he's never around.

Men are made to protect, to provide, and to defend. That's what they do, and most of them do it well when given the opportunity. Unfortunately, you've been told that if women were liberated from the "burden" of caring for home, husband, and children, and men were liberated from the "burden" of producing an income, equality would prevail and life would be grand.

That is a war on human nature that can't be won. Society may change, but people don't.

If you've ever wondered why there are so few "good" (aka marriageable) men these days, the answer is simple: Women and society have made men feel superfluous, which in turn deflated their desire to provide and protect on women's behalf.

Sadly, society doesn't get it. In response to the recent development that women in America make up the majority of the U.S. workforce, Liza Mundy wrote in *The Richer Sex: How the New Majority of Female Breadwinners Is Transforming Sex, Love, and Family* that the traditional family is dead—and that human behavior must change to reflect this fact.

"The rise of women earners will shape human behavior by challenging some of the most primal and hardwired ways men and women see one another. It will alter how we mate, how and when we join together, how we procreate and raise children, and how we pursue happiness. It will reshape the landscape of the heart."[49]

What feminists like Mundy envision is an androgynous world. They want men and women to be virtually indistinguishable—that's why they love the LGBTQ community, where gender is murky. The rest of American women, meanwhile, still want *some form* of a traditional family. It doesn't have to be *Leave It to Beaver*—mine isn't. But the basic structure is the same.

I don't pretend it will be easy to find what you're looking for. I saw a clip on the *Today Show* about Olympic athlete Lolo Jones. She's thirty years old, gorgeous, and a proud virgin. Apparently Lolo had a series of obstacles to overcome in life. She attended eight different schools in an eight-year period while her single mother, Lori, sometimes held two jobs to support her family of six. Lolo's father spent most of her childhood either in the Air Force or in state prison. When Lolo was in the third grade, her family settled in the basement of a Salvation Army church.

To cope, Lolo did two things. One, she concentrated all her energies on track, with the goal of winning an Olympic medal. Two, she committed herself to virginity. Lolo knew that in order to achieve her dreams, both professionally and personally (she wants a traditional family), she would need to keep herself on the straight and narrow. She needed to stay focused—and she did.

The downside, of course, is that it's been hard for Lolo to find a great guy. As I wrote in Part One of this book, guys tend to go where they can get some action. It has always been this way. Today, unfortunately, the "action" is everywhere—which makes it harder to find a man who's willing to commit.

Women like Lolo are the kind of role models young women lack. If Lolo had chosen to remain a victim of her circumstances—and she certainly could have—she would not be where she is today. Lolo Jones is a great example of true female empowerment.

Don't mistake being empowered with being employed. Earning a paycheck is *one* way to feel empowered, but it's not the only way. According to the *Free Online Dictionary*, to *empower* means simply "to equip or supply with an ability; to enable."[50]

The word *empowerment* has been butchered. It's associated almost exclusively with women's independence, as though a woman who can stand on her own and never depend on a man is the arbiter of empowerment.

Look at how the press handled the Tom Cruise and Katie Holmes' split (although you could think of any celebrity split, really). The headlines routinely referred to Katie's newfound "freedom," as though getting divorced and becoming a single mom is a positive, ennobling thing. They even called her a "feminist hero."

The obvious impression left in people's minds is that women are better off without men. They then assume, perhaps unknowingly, that what their mothers told them about not relying on a man was smart.

It wasn't smart at all. It *is* smart to get an education and to develop a marketable skill so you can take care of yourself if need be. But to teach an entire generation of women to think men aren't dependable so women must prepare to be lifelong earners has been utterly disastrous for everyone.

You need an entirely new approach to life and love.

One, assume the best, not the worst, of men. Most men are supremely easy to love and are anxious to take care of their families. The reason it may not seem that way to you is because you're not appreciating that our society has emasculated men. And when men are emasculated, they have no desire to step up on behalf of women and society.

Moreover, if you choose a good man and treat him well, he's not going to leave you. Men are notoriously loyal and tend not to go that route unless they're sexually starved. And that means the problem isn't the man but the marriage itself.

Two, support your husband or fiancé in his career goals because his work will be more linear than yours. That means when you're engaged (or even in a relationship that's headed that way), your guy should not be following you all over the country according to *your* career plans. You should both put his career first since your career plans will likely change once children come along.

Three, don't use the money you do make as a wife to extricate yourself from what may very well be a salvageable marriage. Certainly if you find yourself married to a bum, having money will allow you to escape. But don't rest on your laurels. It's too easy to stop working on your marriage when you know you can cut and run.

That's also a good reason to join bank accounts, by the way. Having a joint bank account lets your husband know you're "all in" and that you view each other as a team. Sadly, many wives today think not joining bank accounts makes them more vulnerable to divorce. They think of it in the same way they think of cohabitation: as insurance against future doom and gloom.

It doesn't work that way. On the contrary, both create a self-fulfilling prophecy. In the same way cohabitation lessens your chances of getting married and staying married, having separate bank accounts keeps intimacy at bay and will create massive conflict in your marriage. The vast majority of my clients, when they first reach out, have separate bank accounts. Their marital conflict is a direct result of having done so.

Don't be like them.

REJECT THE GREEN GRASS SYNDROME

So here's the thing. *You are never going to get everything you want all wrapped up in one man.* It doesn't matter whom you end up with—John Doe or Brad Pitt—there will always be something missing. Always. If this is a phenomenon you can't get your head around, you are not alone. You're suffering from an affliction your generation knows well. It's called the *Green Grass Syndrome.*

The Green Grass Syndrome can apply to any choice we make in life—whether it's which item to order on the menu, which pair of jeans to buy, or which man to marry. I know it's unpleasant to think about marriage in this way, but the process is similar.

When it comes to choosing a husband, you must decide on your non-negotiables—the traits or characteristics you cannot live without—and then forget about everything else. Because the man you pick, no matter who he is, is going to have deficiencies.

And guess what?

So do you.

That will be especially hard for your generation to accept since you've been raised to think you're perfect just the way you are.

"Never settle for less than the best!" you were told. "You *deserve* it." Consequently, young women set their sights insanely high—which means every potential husband winds up appearing substandard.

The struggle to be satisfied is particular relevant to women. As we covered in Step #2, girls today have been raised on the heels of two movements—the feminist movement and the self-esteem movement. These two worldviews are so similar they're impossible to extricate. Feminism tells women, "Your mothers' lives were constrained. Don't live your life the way they did. Reach for the stars instead!" And the self-esteem movement says, "There's no one quite like you. You're *amazing*. Go—seize the world."

The implication is that women are entitled to lives that defy description. They should be out-of-this-world exciting. It's a message that gets delivered to women's doorsteps every day via television, smartphones, and laptops. Programs that portray a female character living a whirlwind life of sex, fantasy, and riches are a dime a dozen. Together, they provide a breeding ground for the Green Grass Syndrome.

Initially, the self-esteem movement seemed harmless. Now you might think, "Why is it bad to encourage young women to shoot for the stars?"

Well, for one thing, it's elitist. The implication is that to shoot for a regular old life or a regular old job somehow constitutes a lesser life. As a result, girls grow up believing recognition and prestige are more important than simply refining a skill set, getting married, and raising a family, or just living by the golden rule.

Even more preposterous is the idea that big careers—which leave zero room for other aspects of life, be it family or friendships or time needed for exercise and relaxation—don't even represent what most women want out of life.

When asked, most women say they want multifaceted lives that offer more time, not more money. Women are not linear in their needs and goals the way men are. They want more out of life than climbing a huge career ladder will allow.

So why do we insist on steering young women in the wrong direction? It should be more than enough to find a loving spouse, raise a couple of great kids, find meaningful work if desired, and be part of a strong community. Research shows this is what makes people happiest anyway.

But the modern generation of women has been convinced that if they don't do something monumental, their lives will be meaningless. They think if they don't marry a smart and successful "hot" guy, they're "settling." As twenty-something Rachel Weight wrote in an article entitled "How *The Notebook* Has Ruined Me": "I think movies like this may have ruined me. Under their influence, I now expect a formula for my romantic life."[51]

Indeed. And that formula—hot Hollywood man/hot Hollywood sex—will lead to some serious disappointment down the road. How many of us can possibly have sex in the manner Noah and Allie did for years on end? You may theoretically know this is impossible, that *The Notebook* is just a movie; but a steady, everyday diet of this stuff is going to find its way into your psyche. There's no way around it.

What women don't realize is that even if they do get everything they think they want, the excitement will be short-lived. Once the high wears off—which it will, as we learned in Step #4—women will want something they've been told all their lives they should have: more. Always, always more.

For those who suffer from the desire for more, the grass *always* looks greener on the other side of the fence. But it isn't. It's just a different shade of green.

Did you see the film *Mona Lisa Smile*? The one set in the 1950s that starred Julia Roberts? Its message is that rather than "just" get married and have babies—which wastes a woman's real talents—women should travel the world, run companies, be sexually liberated, or become president! But whatever she does, she should not become "just" a wife and mother—or housewife, as they called it then.

By liberating themselves from this prism, women were told, they can live lives equivalent to a movie star's.

This narrative was designed to get women to think outside the marriage-and-motherhood box . . . which on its own isn't a bad thing. It simply went too far, as it was later exacerbated by self-esteem rhetoric and an economic boom—in which the drive for "bigger, better, more" became palpable and in which people could get their hands on just about anything they wanted with nothing but a click.

The result is a self-absorbed, narcissistic generation that thinks they're entitled to have what they want, when they want it. And when they don't get it, they can just dump it and start over.

Three excellent books expose this phenomenon. Two are by the same author, psychologist Jean Twenge, and are titled *Generation Me* and *The Narcissism Epidemic*. The other is *NurtureShock* by Po Bronson and Ashley Merryman. Each book points out the harm that excessive praise does to young people. "Sure, [your child] is special," wrote Bronson and Merryman, "but new research suggests that if you tell him that, you'll ruin him. It's a neurobiological fact."[52]

And many women *have* been ruined, for they can't seem to "lower" themselves to an everyday existence. How can the modern woman pick a regular ol' guy and live a regular ol' life when for her entire existence she's been told there's a world out there so exciting that it exceeds her wildest dreams? You do not need a big life to have a valuable life.

The problem with too much choice is that it can cause people to be chronically unsatisfied. No single decision is ever good enough. Moreover, our lax divorce culture makes it easy for husbands and wives to change their minds—and women are particularly susceptible to pulling the trigger. According to the National Marriage Project, two-thirds of all divorces are initiated by women.[53]

The media and your mentors will tell you that's because men just make bad husbands, so women have no choice but to divorce them. Never are women taken to task for what it is they might have done wrong in the marriage or how they might do better.

So, how can you avoid the Green Grass Syndrome? How can you learn to be satisfied?

The first thing is to make an actual list of your wants and needs in a relationship. As you peruse the list, try to think less about what you want and more about what you *don't* want, or what you absolutely can't live without. Since you're never going to get everything on your list, you're going to have to take the good with the bad. You've got to settle into everyday life where humans are flawed, otherwise you'll be perpetually dissatisfied.

When I met my second husband, I was twenty-nine. It was late at night—maybe even morning—and he'd arrived at the bar where I had serendipitously planted myself, despite my reservations about going out earlier that evening. He had just been to a wedding and was wearing a suit with one of those ocean-blue shirts that, at the time, were all the rage. He looked very handsome.

But that only mildly interested me. Obviously, we need to be attracted to someone in order to be interested in him or her—that's a given. But what was on my radar at that point in my life (and on his, apparently) was the desire for children and family. For permanence. Our attraction to each other was a given, but other things took precedence.

In thinking about my future, I knew what I wanted—and more importantly, what I *didn't* want. I knew that if I didn't find a man whose principles and priorities were similar to my own (since I'd failed in this regard the first time around), my marriage wouldn't last.

I also wanted a spouse who was flexible and easygoing, someone who could just as easily go camping as he could attend a black tie event. Finally, I wanted someone who would put family first, who had a strong faith in God, and who was capable of being self-reflective. And, of course, he had to be gainfully employed.

Those were my non-negotiables, but there are plenty of things I don't have. For example (and this is a small thing), I wish my husband did not do everything last minute. I can't tell you how many times he's been *in* the shower when company arrives, and I used to get so mad. Today when people come over and ask where he is, I just smile and say he's in the shower, like it's the most natural thing in the world. Like everyone does that. I've come to accept this part of his personality because there's nothing I can do about it.

My husband can also be very deadpan in his reactions, which leaves me wondering what he really thinks about something. I sometimes find his laid-back demeanor annoying.

But wait. Didn't I say a moment ago that I wanted an easygoing guy? Why yes, I did. So I can hardly complain that my husband's easygoing when that's exactly what I said I wanted.

See how crazy it is? The desire to have everything just the way you'd like it seeks no end. It's just unrealistic to expect your guy (or gal, though I see little evidence of this quality in men) to have all the qualities on your list. That's why I'm suggesting you focus on your must-haves, or the things you can't live without. Once you have those down, the rest you just have to accept. Besides, there are plenty of things your husband's going to wish *you* were that you're not. The trick is not to hold these things against each other.

By the way, not to get all technical here, but there are actually terms for what we're talking about. "Maximizers" are people who obsess over every choice before and after making one, while "satisficers" are content with whatever decision they make. Barry Schwartz argued in *The Paradox of Choice* that satisficers tend to be happier than maximizers because maximizers spend a great deal of time and energy reaching a decision and are often anxious about whatever decision they end up making. Simply put, they're never satisfied.[54]

If you want to be happily married, you're going to have to become a satisficer.

The second thing you need to do is *accept that what matters to you now likely won't mean beans to you down the road.* When you're young and not thinking about bills, kids, schools, or churches, it's easy to overlook the things that will matter later on. This is where maturity comes into play. It takes a big, fat dose of maturity to be able to think beyond tomorrow. What do you envision twenty years from now? Whatever it is, that needs to be at the forefront of your mind when you're deciding whether or not to marry him.

Now I wish I could say the Green Grass Syndrome ends once you decide whom to marry. Unfortunately, it will most likely kick you in the ass down the road.

You'll find your guy, and life will be great—for a while. Maybe even a long while. But at some point along the way, you and your husband will face some very real problems, and it is then that you may find yourself questioning your choice of a husband. Not in a bad, debilitating way (I hope), but in a general way. And when that happens, you may start to notice other people's husbands. After all, it's human nature to compare, and these comparisons happen most when problems arise. You may think to yourself, *Gee, why can't my husband be like that?*

That's when you need to stop.

Don't go any further. When this happens, if it happens, you need to remember what I said at the beginning of this chapter. *No matter whom you marry, if you are a victim of the Green Grass Syndrome, the grass always looks greener on the other side of the fence.* Always.

You need to remember that these things you're noticing, whatever they may be, only appear greener from a distance. In truth, the grass on that other side is just as brown as it is on yours. Assuming this ahead of time allows you to get your mind off the other potential life and put it back on your life, where it belongs.

I truly believe this is where so many women get into trouble. Our divorce culture encourages women to search for something better when they're dissatisfied.

I'm not saying most women treat their marriage with little regard. I'm saying that when the going gets tough, and it will, the culture in which we live helps push women out the door.

You need to understand what our culture won't tell you: When doubt creeps in, that doesn't mean your marriage is doomed, and it doesn't mean you chose the wrong husband. *Everyone* has doubts. Doubt is normal. Doubt is human.

But it won't be debilitating unless you let it.

To avoid this fate, you need a keen awareness of the Green Grass Syndrome—and then you need to reject it. Because once you know these other husbands, or other marriages, or other lives, are no better or worse than yours, your perspective immediately changes. Because the moment you say to yourself, "Hmm . . . I wonder if I'd be better off with that man," or, "I wonder if I'd be happier with that life," you'll remember that that man or life just looks better because it's new.

In reality, both have just as many warts as yours. They're just different warts.

I can't tell you how important it is to understand this once you've made your decision about whom to marry. Honestly, I'd put money on the fact that at some point you're going to ask yourself if you married the right guy. Life is hard, and it's natural to want to bolt when things get tough. Only by avoiding the Green Grass Syndrome will you come out ahead.

Finally, keep in mind what I said about my own marriage: It is not a fairy tale. It has taken an enormous amount of emotional work on my part, as well as on my husband's, to keep our marriage strong. Each of us came to our marriage with baggage: I had a failed marriage behind me, and my husband is a child of divorce. While my husband and I were fortunate to find each other, we didn't rest on our laurels.

Too many people think finding a spouse is about being in the right place at the right time, as if a husband or wife is just "out there" somewhere, waiting to be found—and that once you've found him or her, that's it! Job done.

But that's not how it works.

It is our *attitude*, our views on marriage as society's great stabilizer, that keeps my husband and me chugging along. It's not that we don't have problems that could potentially lead to divorce—everyone does. We're just don't believe there's a better life or a better person out there for us. Things would have to be really, really bad before we'd get divorced. Really bad—not just, "I'm not happy with you anymore" or "You just don't do it for me anymore" bad.

All of which is to say: Decide what you need, and ignore the rest. Match your expectations with reality. When you run into trouble in your marriage—and you will—look inward, not outward. Assume the answer to your problems lies within the marriage, not outside of it. Only then can you solve your problems.

Research shows that most people who get divorced bring the same unresolved issues to their new marriages anyway. That's because the problem wasn't necessarily the marriage, but *the way the couple dealt with the problems* within that marriage. More often than not, a new marriage will present just as many problems as the old.

That's why second marriages have a higher divorce rate than first marriages, and why third marriages have a higher divorce rate than second—and so on. With each divorce, your chances of another divorce increase. The only reason I'm exempt from this statistic is that I didn't have children with my ex. It's the remarriages and the creation of new families, and the attempt to blend them, that problems creep in.

Bottom line: We must stop instilling in women this idea that their lives have in store for them something profound, something magical, something so great it belies description. Unrealistic expectations set up a false reality, and real life can only be disappointing.

It's perfectly normal to wonder if the grass is greener in someone else's backyard, but it isn't normal to believe you've settled for a second-rate life. It isn't normal when this phenomenon consumes you. That kind of thinking comes from cultural conditioning. Only by accepting that you're going to be dissatisfied *to some degree* no matter whom you marry—and by knowing that when this happens, someone else's life will seem more appealing but isn't—will the Green Grass Syndrome stop crippling your life.

And now I'll close with this nugget of wisdom from Schwartz's book:

> *A friend once told me how his minister had shocked the congregation with a sermon on marriage in which he said, flatly that, yes, the grass is always greener. What he meant was that you will encoun-*

ter people who are younger, better looking, funnier, smarter, or seemingly more understanding or empathetic than your wife or husband.

But finding a life partner is not a matter of comparison shopping or "trading up." The only way to find happiness and stability in the presence of seemingly attractive and tempting options is to say, "I'm simply not going there. I've made my decision about a life partner, so this person's empathy or that person's looks really have nothing to do with me. I'm not in the market—end of story."[55]

End of story indeed.

KNOW YOUR BODY

A tragedy has befallen American women. Few other modern crises have been as financially and emotionally devastating as an entire generation of women realizing they missed their opportunity to conceive. Or at least to conceive the natural way.

The most egregious aspect of this phenomenon is that, for many women, this was entirely avoidable. But the truth about fertility has been squelched. No one wants to say to women, "You have a window, ladies. Wait too long, and you'll be sorry." So I'll say it.

Ladies, you have a window. Wait too long, and you'll be sorry.

Here's some sobering news: According to the Human Fertilisation and Embryology Authority, which collects data on roughly fifty thousand fertility treatments performed each year in the UK, nearly *a quarter* of the patients who sought treatments in order to become pregnant between 1991 and 2008 (the average age of the study's patients was thirty-five), experienced "Unexplained Infertility."[56] "Male factors" was a bit higher, at 29.7 percent. But all the other data as to why women couldn't conceive—ovarian failure, endometriosis, etc.—paled in comparison to "Unexplained Infertility."

But there's nothing inexplicable about it. The reason these women can't conceive is because they waited too long.

Mother Nature is a powerful force. If she had her way, most women would become mothers in their teens. (Yikes! Let's not do that . . .) But Mother Nature *closes* the window too. "The likelihood of getting pregnant following IVF or DI treatment is strongly linked to the age of the woman being treated. On average, a woman under thirty-five years old is substantially more likely to conceive than a woman who is older."[57] Once you're over forty, it's nearly impossible—at least without serious and expensive medical intervention.

This seems like basic information women need, don't you think? Yet even doctors won't relay this data. Imagine looking into the eyes of a thirty-nine-year-old woman who's praying for a baby and telling her she's waited too long to conceive. Not gonna happen.

Take Kate, who happens to be someone I know, but there's nothing unusual about her story. Kate took years to get to the altar. Not because she didn't have a boyfriend—she did—but because she was uber-focused on her career. Like so many young women, Kate stayed in school for almost a *decade* as she bounced around from one career concept to another. At thirty-two, she decided to marry her longtime boyfriend. Then she waited another three years to start talking about having kids. Just talking, mind you.

That's when things went south. By the time Kate and her husband got down to business, her body didn't want to cooperate. Kate had several miscarriages. Despondent, she visited her doctor, who told her getting pregnant was not going to be easy. So Kate began fertility treatments. It took five treatments, and thirty thousand dollars, to get one baby. One. When he was born, Kate was thirty-eight. Desperate for another baby, she and her husband depleted their savings account to try to make it happen. It never did.

Same thing happened to Rebecca Walker, daughter of Alice Walker, who wrote *The Color Purple*. Rebecca wrote a compelling article detailing her unfortunate feminist upbringing. Here's a portion of it:

> *As a child, I yearned for a traditional mother. . . . I grew up believing that children are millstones around your neck and the idea that motherhood can make you happy is a complete fairy tale. . . . When I hit my 20s, . . . I could feel my biological clock ticking, but I felt if I listened to it, I would be betraying my mother and all she had taught me. . . . In fact, having a child has been the most rewarding experience of my life. . . . My only regret is that I discovered the joys of motherhood so late—I have been trying for a second child, but so far with no luck.*[58]

Now, to be fair, most women didn't grow up with feminist mothers as strident as Alice Walker. But they did grow up with mothers who implied that marriage and motherhood hold women back. Either that, or they did have traditional mothers but let the culture steer them wrong.

Regardless of the reason, there's so much women need to know about infertility that they don't. Let's begin with the research compiled by Miriam Grossman, MD, a former campus psychiatrist at UCLA. Out of concern for the scores of college girls who showed up at her door for advice about sex and STDs, Grossman designed a pamphlet called Sense & Sexuality. Here's the part on fertility:

> *Seventy-five percent of college freshmen say raising a family is an "essential or very important goal." Yet 55% of younger high-achieving women are childless at thirty-five, and 89% think they'll be able to get pregnant into their forties. This is patently false.*

*It is easiest for a woman to conceive and deliv-
er a healthy child in her twenties. Fertility de-
clines slightly at thirty, and more dramatically at
thirty-five. Waiting rooms of fertility clinics are
packed with health-conscious women who work
out and count calories—they're there because they're
forty years old.*[59]

Prior to the 1960s, women didn't need facts like these because
most women had children in their twenties. Then feminists came
along and told women to pursue a career and delay motherhood as
long as possible.

But women's progress outside the home has meant *regress*
inside the home. Some things in life we can't change, and our
fertility is one of them. We cannot make our bodies do what we
want them to do.

Don't misunderstand. I'm not saying delayed childbirth is a
terrible idea in and of itself. Personally, I think the ideal age to have
a child is in one's mid- to late-twenties. But if women *are* going to
delay motherhood, they need to know the facts—and most don't.
All they see are high-profile women who have babies late in life.
These actresses and television personalities—women like Susan
Sarandon, Brooke Shields, Geena Davis, Salma Hayek, Mariska
Hargitay, Nicole Kidman, and Kelly Preston—help foster the notion, perhaps unwittingly, that motherhood can be chosen in whatever manner and on whatever timetable women choose.

It doesn't work that way. The only reason these women
can do it is because they have a bottomless pit of cash to force
the matter along.

That's why it was a breath of fresh air to read *Desperate Housewives'* Marcia Cross tell *People* magazine that having babies later

in life is "like a miracle." She added, "What I didn't want to do was put out the myth that you can be in your forties and just pop out kids ... It's very, very difficult to get pregnant in your 40s. It's costly and tough on your body and your relationship."[60]

Brooke Shields has been honest as well. "It's important for women to be aware of potential problems and to take control. Two eggs do not an omelette make."[61] And Courteney Cox: "I get pregnant pretty easily, but I have a hard time keeping them."[62]

Kudos to these ladies for telling the truth—really, that's what every celebrity who becomes a mother at a late age should do. These women have a moral obligation to set the record straight; it's one of the trade-offs for being so revered in our Hollywood-obsessed culture.

Unfortunately, comments like theirs get lost in the shuffle. Salma Hayek's claim that "there's no reason women should feel rushed to have a child"[63] is far more commonplace. And it's destructive.

I know the choice to delay motherhood feels liberating since it frees you up to do other things. But remember when I said too much choice can be counterproductive? Twenty-something blogger, Kate Fridkis, who's married but does not have children yet, is a great illustration of just how gut-wrenching choice has become. In an article titled "The Invisible Baby That Follows Me Around," she wrote:

> People ask me, "So are you guys thinking about kids?" That's what happens when you get married. Even in New York City, the land of not-having-to-think-about-kids-until-you're-30. "I think I'll have a baby when I'm thirty, man or not," said one of my friends at a group event. "What?" the other twenty-something women cried. "Thirty? That's too

young! How about thirty-five?" The land of not-having-to-think-about-kids-until-you're-35.

The thing is—I want to have a baby. Sometimes I want to have one RIGHT NOW. I'm a little embarrassed to admit that. Especially since people from NYC read this blog. Sometimes I see a baby and I get that melty feeling that women get when they fit scientifically supported stereotypes. It's like my uterus is talking to me. It's sort of sly and purring. "Come on . . . you know you want one . . . you could have one . . ." And then I go home and stare at the wreckage of the book I'm trying to write, and I feel slightly panicky. And then my brain turns to steel and snaps at my uterus to please be quiet until you have something worthwhile to say. I have things to do. Lots of things. I have to make something of myself.

That damn clock.[64]

Then Fridkis added this nugget of wisdom: "In the world I live in, 'making something of yourself' means your career. In my mom's world, it means your family. This is all very confusing." Translation: America's values are so screwed up that women now feel they must *justify their existence* by being employed.

That's exactly what I mean when I say the culture is against you.

Bottom line: Know your body. You do have some time, but you don't have all the time in the world. If you wait too long, you will feel rushed—and that can make it harder to conceive. (It can also mean making a poor choice of husband.) I've heard so many stories about women who tried desperately to get pregnant, only to end up adopting because they thought they couldn't get pregnant, and then—wham!—they got pregnant. Our bodies don't perform on command.

That's why it's best to start thinking in your twenties about when you want children. You don't have to *do* anything about it—you just need to be thinking about it, as opposed to living day-by-day and giving it no thought whatsoever because you think you're invincible.

When it comes to having babies, there's a window. And that window isn't just about the ability to conceive; it's about the ability to conceive a healthy child. The older women are, the more likely they are to have a child with Down syndrome. And just recently, researchers in Iceland found that older fathers transmit more genetic mutations—such as schizophrenia and autism—to their offspring, and this effect grows with each year of age.

The good news is, there's no cap on women's desire to accomplish most of what they want out of life. Women today have fewer children than ever and simultaneously live longer lives. You just can't do everything all at once. The key is to think long-term. Do *not* live in the moment. Think. Plan. Prepare. Decide.

And when things don't go exactly as planned (and they won't), be flexible. Reorganize and regroup. Do what you need to do. But always, always have a plan. Living moment to moment is what causes so many women to wake up one day and realize their window to conceive, or even to get married, came and went. They thought they had all the time in the world. They didn't.

You don't either.

THERE'S NO SUCH THING AS WORK-FAMILY BALANCE

So now we've arrived at the most pressing issue for marriage-minded women: how to "balance" work and family. This is a subject close to my heart, and I hate the way the media portray it. Whenever they discuss it, either on the news or in films and sitcoms, it's almost always framed within the context of balance.

But *balance* is the wrong word. *Balance* means "a state of equilibrium, or an equal distribution of weight." It refers to emotional stability, calm behavior, and judgment, etc. I can assure you none of these meanings comes close to describing what it's like to "balance" work and family.

When mothers work outside the home, the distribution of weight is never even, and emotions run high. Where do you think the concept of mommy guilt came from? Or how about women's stress?

These terms are new in relation to motherhood—and they exist as a result of women trying to care for children, particularly young children, *while at the same time* pursue demanding careers. "It's just like any working mom's dilemma. It's tough. It's a balancing act. You put them first and then you have all these other things you have to do, things you have to give your time to as well, and you have to make sure they're okay in the process," Jennifer Lopez responded when asked why she left *American Idol.*[65]

You need to understand something no one wants to say: If you attempt to raise your kids, particularly when they're babies and toddlers, while at the same time working full-time and year-round, guilt will never stop tormenting you.

That's your serotonin talking. No man, employer, or poorly designed government is keeping you from balancing work and family. The reason you can't do it is because it isn't possible to do. It's like trying to be a doctor and a lawyer simultaneously: They're both full-time, taxing endeavors that eat up your time and invade your mind.

You have to prioritize.

That's not how the issue is framed in the media. If you read women's magazines, you'll find scores of articles devoted to helping mothers try to alleviate their guilt, justify their guilt, or get rid of their guilt.

Ever since the mass exodus of mothers from the home, women with children who work full-time have been consumed with guilt. That's because if you're not there to take care of your children most of their waking hours, you are going to feel bad about it. It's not any more complicated than that.

You know your baby needs you because you can see it for yourself every time he cries as you pry him off your body to hand him over to hired help. Why do this to yourself if you don't have to?

(And no, most married mothers don't "have" to work. More on that in a moment.)

The only way to avoid the kind of debilitating guilt that eats women alive is to not try and do everything and be everything all at once. Women must stop living their lives as if they're going to die tomorrow and won't be able to get everything done. There's plenty of time. Relax.

This might sound silly, but let's compare the work-family dilemma to ordering a meal at a restaurant. When you sit down, everything on the menu looks great: the steak, the scallops, the salmon. Your mouth is salivating over all the options. And while in reality you could order it all, you'd be too full to enjoy the whole thing. You'd only get to experience bits and pieces of each. And who wants just three bites of a fifty-dollar steak?

So what can you do? Order one meal one night, and come back another night to try the next one. It's as simple as that. You make a choice, and you make the most of it. Making choices is part of life. You can't go to every party. You can't go on every vacation. You can't go to every college. You have to choose.

Most married mothers who work outside the home full-time and year-round are making a choice. They are *choosing* to focus the bulk of their time and attention on their jobs, as opposed to on their homes and their children.

They're not balancing anything. They're juggling.

Jugglers never have both or all of the balls in the air at one time. When one is up, the other is down. To juggle means "to alternately toss and catch something," or "to have difficulty holding more than one thing at a time." That's the opposite of balance.

Ironically, to juggle (according to Merriam-Webster) also means "to practice deception," or "to manipulate in order to deceive." In a previous book, *The Flipside of Feminism*, I devoted an entire chapter to the argument that multitasking is a fraud and referred to a great book called *The Myth of Multitasking*. The message of this book is that the human brain is like a computer: It is capable of focusing on only one thing at a time. Switching back and forth between different tasks cannot overcome the brain's inability to process two sets of data simultaneously. Thus, multitasking is a myth.

I'm not saying you can't do *any* two things at once. You may, for example, be able to put dinner together while helping your second grader with homework. But the fancier the recipe and the more complicated the homework, the less successful you will be at either one.

Juggling two or more activities that require mental acuity is not the same as doing laundry and talking on the phone. And I've even messed that up. (My particular favorite is watching people grocery shop while having a conversation with their friends on their iPhones. The few times I've attempted this, I invariably returned home with the wrong items.)

Mothers who work full-time and have children at home, particularly young children, are doing two things at once, half as well. They are becoming jacks-of-all-trades and masters of none, which is why they're guilt-ridden and stressed out all the time. It's also the reason why, historically, women waited until their children were older and more independent before taking outside jobs.

For years I've been banging the pot loudly about how critical it is to be physically and emotionally present for one's children and how impossible it is to have it all at one time. And when I do, some people ask how I manage my own life. Or, if they're mad at what I have to say, they'll tell me I'm a hypocrite.

Here I am, they say, a woman who clearly has it all. Yet I insist that 'having it all' isn't possible. I tell other women they should stay home, they say; yet I traipse all over the country giving speeches, or I sit at my computer all day while my children fend for themselves.

These folks imagine a gotcha moment: *Aha!* they think. *Suzanne must have a well-paid nanny in the background. Either that, or there's some other secret she's not sharing. Maybe her kids have been raised on the idiot box, or her mother raised her kids for her. Something's not right.*

The reason people make these assumptions is twofold. One, they're assuming I have it all—and I don't. My writing career is exactly half what it could be if I did not have a husband and children. (And that's as it should be.) Two, things are never as they appear. Hence, the assumptions.

My argument has always been the same. Women who are looking to combine work and family should make clear and purposeful choices early on with this goal in mind. They must also recognize that children have needs, and that those needs must be met. If you do this early on, as I did, you will wind up having both family and career in piecemeal fashion, over the course of your lifetime—sans guilt and stress.

Sadly, women aren't encouraged when they're young to give any thought to marriage and motherhood. Instead, they map out their lives according to their career plans and let the chips fall where they may when it comes to the rest.

Moreover, their perception of "having it all" doesn't mean having a little bit of this and a little bit of that—the way it does to me. It means being able to accomplish *anything they want, to any degree they desire,* while still maintaining a normal, healthy family life.

That's impossible. Literally impossible. No one can do this. No one has yet. Why would you be any different?

The women in your life lied. You can't, in fact, do or be anything you want if you also plan to get married and have kids. Some careers just won't be an option, particularly the powerful and lucrative ones. You can choose them, if you wish, but not without ramifications. Becoming a surgeon, for instance, will invariably pose a problem for women who want children. There's no way around it.

That was the crux of the hoopla surrounding the article in *The Atlantic* entitled "Why Women Still Can't Have It All." The author, Anne-Marie Slaughter, pointed out what I've been hammering home for years: Women can't have it all, not at once. Life is about trade-offs, and my life is certainly no different.

It may not look that way from the outside. After all, people see me on TV or hear me on the radio and assume I have some highfalutin career. I also do speaking engagements on occasion, so the assumption is that I'm routinely flying all over the country (or world). I was interviewed recently, and one of the hosts opened the segment saying, "So you travel the country talking about . . ."

So let's begin there. I *do not* "travel the country." My speaking engagements, as well as TV spots, are few and far between—they are not the bulk of what I do. They also require only between a few hours and one day to accomplish. The main thing I do when I'm not busy being a mom is write.

Writing happens to be a career I can control: I work from home; I'm not at the mercy of a boss; I can say no to anything that conflicts with my personal life; and I can work my entire schedule around my children's needs. So while on paper I'm what people call a "working mother," I'm a terrible example of one. Because of *very purposeful choices* I've made along the way, I have been my children's sole caregiver. Along with their father, of course, but he works a regular full-time job.

I recognize that not everyone can work from home and that in this way I'm fortunate. However, becoming a writer was not my original plan. I was going to, and did, become a teacher. But I ultimately decided even that career, for me anyway, would conflict with motherhood. That's because if I'm going to do something, I can't do it halfway and thus did not keep teacher's hours. So I changed course.

I made other choices as well. I have two children instead of three or four—though that was partly because I had my second child at thirty-five, and he was a handful. Still, I *could* have tried for a third. I also divorced one man I feared would not be around much and married a man whose career goals were more family friendly and who's therefore more available on the home front.

Do not underestimate any of these choices. The number of children you want, the kind of man you marry, and the type of work you choose to do are all critical factors in your ability to "have it all."

That said, "having it all" is really the wrong phrase—perhaps even the wrong goal. If by using this phrase you mean that over the course of your lifetime you will have been successful both professionally and personally, great. But you can't be president, or fly to the moon, or even make it to the corner office if being a hands-on, get-your-hands-dirty kind of mother is nonnegotiable. For me, it was. It is.

Bottom line: How visible I am as a writer and speaker at any given time depends entirely on where my children are in their development, both physically and emotionally. When they were babies and toddlers, I dropped out of sight completely. Once they were in school, I worked part-time hours. Now that they're grown and gone, I've upped the ante considerably.

I do have one leg up, however, in that my husband works from home. And while that is a strain of its own, it has unquestionably allowed me to pursue my writing career more easily. I simply could not do what I do without two things: my husband's steady, reliable income, and the flexibility of both our jobs. Whom you choose to marry really does matter.

If you want to be successful at home and at work, begin by recognizing that you've been sold a script that won't work. As long as you have some form of employment on your plate when you are raising children, you will never feel genuinely relaxed—or, in some cases, even content.

You cannot blame your husband, your employer, or the government for this predicament. If you don't want to feel this way, don't attempt to work outside the home at all—or at the very least cut your work load in half—when you have young children. Though the media would like you to believe otherwise, there are millions of women who choose this path.

When you remove the work-related task from the equation, when you focus exclusively on the needs of your children and the home, *which take up a considerable portion of your time no matter how well you organize your time*, your attitude toward motherhood is welcomed rather than resented. You're just a whole different kind of mother when you don't have someplace you have to be, or something else you need to get done.

The only way to feel good about performing any task, whether it's work-related or home-related, is to give it your undivided attention.

I assume you'd rather enjoy your children than resent them. If so, throw the concept of having it all in the trash, where it belongs. Instead, create realistic expectations for what you can accomplish during this season of your life, and find a job or career that's flexible. If you can't find anything that works, let it go. Don't work.

The truth is, most women didn't do what I did. They were too busy living day to day, or they succumbed to the culture's message that women should put career at the center of their lives and fit everything else in around that. As a result, women end up at the mercy of their jobs. They made choices based on the assumption that they'd always be in the workforce. I didn't do that, and it made all the difference.

I mention this only because you *do* have options; it's just that no one presented them to you. You grew up hearing that it's impossible financially for the average married woman to stay home with her children, and that just isn't true. In fact, the majority of married mothers who are home are *not* rich.

When both parents try to bring home a paycheck *and* plan for and prepare seven days' worth of meals; do the dishes; pay the bills; mow the lawn; paint the shutters; fix the leaky faucet; go to Target; do the laundry; pick up the dry cleaning; take out the trash (on the right day at the right time so it doesn't get backed up and stink up your house and garage); go to Home Depot; shop for clothes; take the kids to the doctor; return phone calls; maintain their friendships; go to the gym . . . oh, and raise helpless babies to become healthy, mature, responsible adults, the result can be only chaos.

People can spin it any way they want, but that's what this life represents: chaos.

Raising a family was never meant to be a sideline occupation done with whatever leftover time parents had to offer. The only reason Americans don't look at it this way today is because our views on parenting have changed. We're too focused on what adults want rather than on what children need.

Remember when I talked about the 1960s cultural shift away from the universal moral order and onto moral relativity, or doing what's best for the individual? The mass exodus of mothers from the home is a quintessential example of this phenomenon.

The universal moral order demanded people do what's best for the family. With its opposite value, moral relativity, the knee-jerk reaction to working motherhood is indifference. The decision about whether or not to stay home and raise one's children is viewed as no different from the choice between vanilla or chocolate.

When a pregnant Melissa Mayer was named the new Yahoo! CEO, scores of articles were written about it. The theme was that society shouldn't have any opinion about the fact that Mayer says she won't need maternity leave. That would be judgmental, and making value judgments is the ultimate taboo in modern America.

But Ms. Mayer's decision to give birth and then return to her former life as though nothing happened would have been a shocking action, let alone thought, prior to the feminist movement. Our mothers and grandmothers didn't have the burden of "deciding" whether or not they wanted to stay home with their children. It was assumed they would. It was understood that giving birth is the *least* of a mother's job, that it's what comes afterward that matters.

There are two ways to view the mass exodus of mothers from the home: as a boon for women's "rights," or as a tragedy for children, families, and society as a whole. I view it as the latter.

But since the culture makes it clear that the former view is the correct or only view to have, it makes sense that mothers who are on the fence about whether or not to stay home would need some incentive to make that choice. They need to understand that it *is* possible, and why it's important to do so.

Others *know* they want to stay home but need to convince their fiancés or husbands that it's the right thing to do. That's how destructive the narrative has been.

If you run into this problem, here's what you tell your guy. First, it is rarely economically sound for both parents to work full-time—at least when children are young. Two, the needs of children, especially babies, are not being met. A lot of parents think babies don't require much and assume nothing of consequence happens until they're older. That just isn't true. The early years are critical for bonding and for emotional development. When these needs aren't met, the void lasts throughout adulthood and creates problems in adult relationships.

"Americans have devalued parenting, and specifically motherhood, and are creating emotionally impoverished young people who have difficulty in sustaining intimate relationships and functioning as independent adults."[66]

We don't hear much about this, yet it's vital not only to our children's health but to the health of our nation. The emotional well-being of our children is at stake. The ability to trust, to empathize, and to be intimate in our relationships aren't traits we're born with, like personality traits. They're learned.

In the first three years of life.

Accepting this is a tall order for Americans who've been conditioned to embrace daycare as harmless, but we ignore this lie at our peril. When babies fail to bond, it's bad news for all of us. The loss of self-worth these individuals experience from having either been ignored or passed around from caregiver to caregiver stays with them for life. When babies don't have one primary caregiver, preferably the mother, who tends to the baby the majority of his or her waking hours, they run the risk of failing to bond.

"Young children do not form a strong attachment to a person they see little of, no matter how kindly the person is or how superlative the quality of time spent together," wrote William and Wendy Dreskin, coauthors of *The Day Care Decision* and former owners/directors of a daycare center.[67]

Indeed, parents need to be physically and emotionally present in their children's lives if they expect to raise emotionally healthy children who have their own strong relationships later on. When babies are separated from their mothers (or from their one primary caregiver) for long periods of time, they may never learn to trust or to love.

This is a delicate subject. It's one of those topics we're not supposed to talk about so that mothers who don't stay home in the early years don't feel bad. But there's so much misinformation about nonmaternal care. Americans are truly in the dark when it comes to children's needs.

The main thing to know is this: Substitute, nonmaternal care for children, even babies, isn't harmful *if used sparingly*. It's the every-day, all-day or most-of-the-day substitute care that's the problem.

By "sparingly," I mean a few hours here and there, the same way you might leave a baby or toddler at home with a sitter. Three days a week at a child care center, from eight to five, does not constitute "sparingly." A baby who attends daycare five days a week for three hours a day is actually better off than the baby who attends daycare three days a week from eight to five. That's because it's the number of hours *at one time* that matters. It's just too disruptive to babies' sleep and food schedules, and to the bonding process.

There's tons of information about this subject, if you're interested—it's actually quite fascinating. I first studied it in college. Boston University had an accredited daycare in its school of education, and I would go behind one of those windows where the toddlers couldn't see me but I could see them, and I would study their interactions with their mothers when they dropped them off.

I also worked in numerous childcare environments and as a nanny during the summers. But it wasn't until I became a mother and wrote my first book, *The Two-Income Trap* (which was essentially about the needs of children) that I became passionate about the issue. I wish all parents were privy to this information. If they were, I think they'd make very different choices about their child care arrangements.

To be clear, this isn't about mom and baby being joined at the hip—I'm not a spokesperson for attachment parenting. What I am saying is this:

If you disappear from your baby's view every day, all day—or even most of the day—he will bond with the person in whose care you left him. Babies attach themselves to whomever they see the most of. You've probably heard about or know of working mothers who become jealous of their nannies. That's why.

I'm also not suggesting daycare shouldn't exist. But by opening it up to anyone who wants to use it, by having it become a *way of life* rather than a last resort, it fails to be effective. The quality of daycare matters, yes. But quality can exist only when the supply exceeds the demand. Right now we have the reverse. No large-scale bureaucratic system can possibly do for children what parents have historically done for free. It's impossible.

This is an uncomfortable truth, to be sure. But the only reason you don't know about the perils of full-time, year-round childcare is because the media won't report it, or even acknowledge it. As Bernard Goldberg pointed out in his book *Bias*, the women in the media drop their children off with someone else for twelve or more hours a day, every day—they're hardly in a position to be objective. Facing this subject would make them feel bad.

Which means unless you have firsthand experience working with babies and toddlers or have a degree in child development, unless you've actively researched the issue, unless you've stayed home with your children and really paid attention to the bonding process, there's no way you'd know any of this.

I'm telling you this because I don't want you to have regrets. Embracing the cultural trend regarding motherhood, the one that says, "Take a short break and then get back to the office," means giving something up you cannot get back. You have one chance—one—to be with your children in the early years, not just for the sake of bonding, but for your own joy and satisfaction as well.

So with all that in mind, let's get back to the burning question, the one that almost every woman wants to know: How do you combine raising a family with the pursuit of a career?

First, decide how many children you want. Because the more children you have, the longer it will be before you feel comfortable turning your attention away from the home. It will also be harder to do pursue a career the more children you have.

Second, you have to prioritize by deciding what you value more: having a strong marriage and raising physically and mentally healthy kids, or being highly successful in your career. You will not get all that; something must give.

Third, determine what you want your day-to-day life to look like. If you want to *not* feel stressed out or guilt-ridden—and if you want to live a calm, rather than a chaotic, lifestyle—you're going to have to change the way you think. Start looking at your life as one long journey in which you have plenty of time to do what you want to do but in piecemeal fashion, rather than all at once.

Fourth, choose a flexible career. Because if you pursue a career path that takes you away from home too much, you are going to be unhappy. (And yes, if you missed the boat on these things early on, you can still switch gears. Plenty of people change jobs or careers or lifestyles later in life.)

Look at Oprah Winfrey. Here's a woman whose professional goals were so high the only way for her to achieve them was to give up marriage and motherhood altogether.

Sugar Rautbord, a fellow Chicagoan who knew Oprah long before she became a millionaire media mogul, told biographer

Kitty Kelley, "[Oprah] figured out early that the only way to have a successful career and make money—big money—was to delete husbands and children and carpools from life's agenda."[68] Oprah Winfrey eats, sleeps, and breathes work—there's very little time for anything else. That is the one and only way anyone reaches those heights.

Any woman who wants that kind of life is free to go out and get it. But when most women think honestly about their lives, a life vacant of family—not to mention all the other facets of life that get lost in the shuffle (exercise, friendships, cooking, free time, etc.)—is not what they want.

This is a sore point for feminists, who insist women earn less than men due to workplace discrimination. The truth is that most women *choose* to make family the focus of their lives. For most women, their job is not the reason they get out of bed every morning. *That's* why they earn less than men.

Keep in mind the media will say that if you don't start working at twenty-two and not stop until you're sixty-five—you know, like men do—you'll be at a disadvantage. But that depends on your view of what it means to be "disadvantaged."

If you measure success by how successful you are professionally, then yes, you'll be at a disadvantage. If, however, your definition of success includes having strong and healthy family, then you're not at a disadvantage at all, are you?

The good news is that it's much easier for women to sequence their lives today. Technological advances provide enormous flexibility, allowing women to work from home or keep themselves engaged in the world outside their doorstep.

I can't tell you how important it is that you marry a man who understands this stuff—because those who've fallen for feminist dogma, even unknowingly, have a different take on work and family matters. Again, men have been just as conditioned as women to believe babies don't need their mothers. Moreover, the culture insists that children whose mothers don't like staying home are better off in daycare.

That is one of our culture's great lies. As renowned psychiatrist John Bowlby once said, "A home must be very bad before it can be bettered by a good institution."[69] Children in low-income families, where stability is lacking or drugs are rampant, is one thing. A middle-class family with a mom and a dad in which the mother is simply bored is something else. Children don't care if their mothers are happy or self-actualized. They just want them around.

(By the way, I feel compelled to point out that one of the reasons at-home motherhood has become "boring" for some is precisely *because* so many mothers have left home for the workplace. Had they not, raising babies and toddlers would not be so taxing. Women would have other mothers around to help them and to provide some much-needed comic relief. That's the real meaning of the phrase "it takes a village.")

It has been my observation that most women determine— even if it takes them years to figure out—that they want marriage and motherhood to be the center of their lives. When you're young, you don't have babies on your mind. I get that. But because you live in a culture that assumes you can't—or won't want to—stay home when the time comes, you have to be someone who thinks outside the box. You have to ask yourself while you're still young—in college is ideal—what it is that you want out of life.

You'll also have to ignore your professors, most of whom are feminist thinkers. Universities are supposed to be genuinely liberal, or open to all schools of thought. But they're not. They preach leftist politics all day long, and the most popular branch is feminism. The more prestigious the school, the more pronounced the feminism.

Which means at the very moment women are mapping out their futures, they're being inundated with feminist propaganda. Rather than get the kind of guidance I'm giving you, which incorporates *all* the different aspects of a woman's life, women get the singular message that their careers will, and should, be the focus of their lives.

It is a philosophy most women come to regret.

In 2007, the National Bureau of Economic Research released this finding: "As women have gained more freedom, more education, and more economic power, they have become less happy."[70] While the authors are careful not to blame feminism directly, they did write this: "As women's expectations move into alignment with their experiences, this decline in happiness may reverse."[71]

Why did women's expectations change in the first place? Because they've been groomed to reject their womanhood. Here's a great example of the message college students absorb.

In 2011, one of the most powerful women in America, Facebook COO Sheryl Sandberg, delivered the commencement address at Barnard College, an all-girls school. During her speech, she offered the graduates the typical feminist/self-esteem message: that there's an amazing world out there, just waiting for women to make their mark. She told the graduates they should stop at nothing to achieve their dreams.

There was no mention of what these young women's futures will actually look like down the road: no talk of husbands or children; no talk of how their priorities will change; no talk of anything but their bombastic future careers.

Then Sandberg chimed in with her larger message regarding social change. She assured the graduates that women have a long way to go to achieve "equality" and offered her vision for America.

"A world where men ran half our homes and women ran half our institutions would be just a much better world," she said.

She prefaced this by saying, "To solve this generation's central moral problem, which is gender equality[,] [w]e need women at all levels, including the top, to change the dynamic, reshape the conversation, to make sure women's voices are heard and heeded, not overlooked and ignored."[72]

Putting aside for a moment Sandberg's shocking assertion that America's *central moral problem* is gender equality (really?), she also told the graduates to "lean in" to their jobs until the last possible moment. "Do not leave before you leave. Do not lean back; lean in. Put your foot on that gas pedal and keep it there until the day you have to make a decision."[73] That decision being, of course, whether or not to leave the workforce to take care of your baby.

This is terrible advice for young women! Women like Sandberg are not the kind of mentors marriage-minded women need. Femininsts like Sandberg are personally vested in getting women to stay in the workforce full-time and year-round on a permanent basis. This allows feminists to push progressive policies that benefit them, not you or your family.

Indeed, feminists have an agenda—and your well-being isn't it.

Sheryl Sandberg is merely assuaging her own grief. Married with two young children, she admits to feeling guilty being away from her children most of their waking hours. "I feel guilty working because of my kids. I do. I feel guilty," she announced at a TED conference.[74] At one point she glossed over what it's like to have her toddler son pulling on his mother's leg, begging her not to go to work—as if that's something a mother should just "get over."

That tugging is the perfect metaphor for the greater tug women feel between their independent selves and their nurturing selves. Very few women are immune to it. But rather than address this conflict head-on, women like Sandberg encourage women to ignore their nurturing side and dismiss their children's needs.

I'm encouraging you to do the opposite.

Sandberg's directive does introduce a bigger question, though—one with which so many Americans, not just women, grapple: What does it mean to be successful?

I personally believe most people instinctively know that success isn't something one deposits in a bank. We're not here on this earth for the money we make or the fame we achieve. We're here for the relationships we build.

That's why marrying a man who's on your side when it comes to the work/life dilemma—deciding whether and how much to work outside the home once children come along—cannot be underestimated.

At the very least, you should know that mothering is hard work. More than hard, actually—it will rock your world. The last thing you need as a mother, particularly a new mother, is the added stress of a full-time job.

Motherhood can be joyous, but only if you aren't rushing off someplace all the time. The moment you're in a rush, the resentment will start to build. Don't let it.

Iris Krasnow said it best in *Surrendering to Motherhood*: "Don't let your profession be an obstacle to knowing and loving your family."[75]

DECIDE TO STAY

First, a caveat: Sometimes divorce is necessary. There are some marriages that must be dissolved for obvious reasons, such as chronic addiction or abuse. Mental illness can also wreak havoc on a marriage.

But in 1969, something happened that changed our view of divorce forever. Ronald Reagan, who was governor of California at the time, signed the nation's first no-fault divorce legislature. All but five states adopted similar bills and, unsurprisingly, divorces skyrocketed.

Reagan later told his son it was "one of the worst mistakes" he ever made in public office because while the intent was good, no-fault divorce opened to the door to the casual and easy divorce culture we have today. The only "grounds" a couple needs to get a divorce today are "irreconcilable differences."

That's a serious can of worms we opened.

Here are some facts to shock us into reality. Research by sociologist James H. Fowler found that if a sibling divorces, we are 22 percent more likely to get divorced ourselves. And when our friends get divorced, it's even more influential: People who had a divorced friend were *147 percent* more likely to get divorced than people whose friends' marriages were intact.[76] Divorce, it appears, is contagious.

There's more. Studies show that, of all divorcing couples, roughly half are open to staying *together if someone could show them how to do so.*

That's a critical piece of information. It tells us millions of marriages are indeed salvageable, and being silent about it does none of us any good. It merely perpetuates the problem.

If I had my way, I'd like to be able to say something like this: "If you do all these things, you will live happily ever after ..." But I can't say that. What I *can* do is tell you a few things that will definitely help keep divorce at bay.

The first is to faithfully follow Step #1: *Ignore the culture and live an examined life.* Because when it comes to getting married and staying married, the culture will steer you wrong. Every single time.

To wit, not long ago I was perusing the magazine section at an airport gift shop and noticed that headline after headline touted the single life for women. Being single is no longer considered a temporary state but something to which women should aspire.

Women's magazines in particular are geared to this demographic, as are sitcoms and dramas. The programs repeatedly make fun of men and of husbands. Even morning news programs chime in.

When a nation of women see high-profile women basking in the single life and treating their husbands with disrespect or even disdain, eventually they assume this is normal behavior. Before you know it, they start doing the same thing.

As I stared at these magazines, the first thing I thought of was how easy it is to lure people away from the more challenging road (marriage) and steer them toward the easy road (singlehood). It's human nature to travel the path of least resistance—and being single is unquestionably the path of least resistance. The choice to love and to commit to another person for a lifetime is, as writer and activist Maggie Gallagher once wrote, "a much higher ideal than choosing not to."[77]

Let's face it. Being single doesn't ask people to look in the mirror and face their weaknesses in order to become better people. It doesn't require someone to derail his or her plans to accommodate the needs of others. It doesn't expect people to learn the art of patience because they won't need to. Being single doesn't ask much of anyone. Singles can live however they see fit, with zero compromise.

The second thing you can do to keep divorce at bay is to *assume it isn't an option*. Entering a marriage knowing you can always get out of it dramatically affects the way you approach the marriage itself. If you're depending on a means to relieve you of your commitment, you will very likely take advantage of it.

Change your attitude, and you will change the outcome. Assume there's no way out, and your chances of success improve exponentially. Remember what Barry Schwartz wrote? "When we can change our minds about decisions, we are less satisfied with them. When a decision is final, we engage in a variety of psychological processes that enhance our feelings about the choice we made relative to the alternatives."[78]

This psychological process applies to any choice we make. Whether you're deciding which car, television, or jeans to buy, or whether you're deciding whom to marry, make your decision as though you have no other option—as though it were your one and only shot. I cannot stress the significance of this attitude enough. It really is the whole enchilada.

When my husband and I have a conflict, even a big one, the prospect of divorce never enters our minds. If we gave ourselves this wiggle room, it would absolutely change the way we approach the problem. The best thing to do is accept going into a marriage

that you're going to have problems and that divorce is not the answer to those problems. If you can do that, you're well on your way
to a successful marriage.

Not long ago, I had a conversation with a sixty-something wife
and mother named Sally. Sally has been married to her husband for
forty-four years, and when I asked her what she thinks the problem
is with the modern generation—why they can't get the marriage
thing right—she didn't hesitate. "They don't know what a vow is."
Everything, she said, is disposable. If something isn't working, people throw it out.

Here's an idea to get you thinking outside the cultural box.
When you find Mr. Right and you've been married for some time,
pretend you're both stranded on an island. Assume you have no other
choice but to work things out, and see if this doesn't change the way
you approach your relationship. Clearly, you're not stuck. The point
is to do the psychological work that's necessary to stay together.

All I'm suggesting, really, is that you start to look at choice in
a whole new light. Today choice is hailed as the be-all and end-all.
"It's all about choice," we're told. Without endless options, where
would women be?

The real answer: likely better off.

Choice isn't all it's cracked up to be. In and of itself, it's good.
But too much choice *can* be bad, as I wrote earlier. When people
have too much choice, says Schwartz, "bad stuff happens."[79] First,
people become paralyzed. With so many options before them,
people "can't pull the trigger." Instead of feeling liberated, they become immobilized.

Too many choices cause people to develop inertia. They become so overwhelmed they don't know which choice to make. And
those who *are* able to make a choice from the endless array of options before them often choose badly. "People make bad decisions

even in simple environments. Just imagine how difficult the decisions are when the environments get complex."[80]

Finally, those who do end up choosing from all the options and choose *well* tend to become dissatisfied down the road. Choice has a bell curve, says Schwartz. People need to figure out for themselves at what point in the "choice space" they can derive the benefits of choice without the psychological loss. They need to find "the sweet spot."[81]

This process can be applied to any choice we make, including whom to marry. When people get divorced and remarry, unless the first choice was exceptionally bad (and certainly that happens), they end up with the same bell curve of happiness. Unfortunately, many people who get divorced don't change their thinking when they enter marriage the second time—which is one of the reasons second marriages are more precarious than first marriages.

At some point, people need to find their "sweet spot" or they'll end up divorced again and again. Either that, or they'll just give up and stay single. Remember: Doubting your choice is perfectly normal. *Everyone does.* There is nothing wrong with you if, on some off day, you can't remember why the heck you married your husband in the first place.

Take actress Kathleen Kinmont, who wrote an article for the *HuffPost* titled, "The 'Do I Really Need a Man?' Checklist." Here's a portion of that article:

> *It's been six months since my third husband moved out. After noting all the feelings and extra workload, I've decided to make a personal checklist of things I need from a man and things I don't . . .*

A few days after the ex moved out, I was so filled with anxiety thinking, "How am I going to manage taking care of the back and front yard by myself?" Thankfully, I was driving by a gardener when this heart palpitation started. I gasped, flagged him down, got his card and gave him my address. The next day he and his partner showed up, and what took my ex all weekend, every weekend, took them half an hour on a Thursday morning. They mowed and blew all my worry into the "yard waste only" can, and I was able to sleep like a baby again.

Check off "I need a man to take care of the yard."

So what about sex? I love it. I think it's really important. I just don't feel like I need a partner to help me pull it off. Certainly with all of the STDs out there, I'm not interested in getting anything else I don't already have.

Check off "I need a man for sex." Just keep the electricity bill paid and all is good.

Speaking of bills . . . do I really need a man to help me pay for them? No. I need a job to help me pay my bills. So to all you women out there in a good marriage or a bad one, get a paying job. It will help if things go awry. As soon as I get one, I'll check it off the list.

I guess the last thing would be companionship. Can I just say that I'm chock full of it? I am on hyper over-load with relationships. I have a wonderful fami-ly and great close friends that I barely have enough time for. I have more "friends," thanks to Facebook, than I know what to do with.

I know that now is the time to fall in love with me, and remind myself that I was a whole person before I met "my other halves or quarters." I just have to fill in my fear with trust, and have the faith that exclaims, Yes, I am enough, and I can do this without a man as my guide or as my barometer of success.[82]

This attitude, or some form of it, is precisely how many wom-en today have been taught to view men and marriage. It's also the attitude that's portrayed in the media, thus perpetuating the notion that it's perfectly normal to think this way.

Meanwhile, the truth lies buried: Ms. Kinmont is broken. Her conclusion after all that pain and heartache is that she needs to fall in love with *herself.* How sad is that?

I can't tell you how many men I hear from who want to be married but who are surrounded by women whose attitudes are similar to Kinmont's. I mentioned before that two-thirds of all di-vorces are initiated by women. There are only two ways to read this: Most men make terrible husbands, or many, many women don't know how to be married.

My experience as a coach tells me it's the latter.

I want you to consider a time in your life when you truly com-mitted to something. When you said you were going to do it and you followed through, no matter how hard it was. Maybe you ran a half marathon, went on a diet, or penned a book.

There were probably times when you felt like giving up, but how thankful are you that you powered through? That your word was your bond? I could be wrong, but my gut tells me that those moments when you made the decision to stay committed probably ended up being among the most rewarding moments of your life.

Marriage is like riding a bicycle: You don't fall off unless you stop pedaling.

Don't stop pedaling. Decide to stay.

FIND GOD

There's no way to write a book about marriage and leave God out of the equation. That's a big subject, though; so I'm going to do my best to address it in just a few pages—and in a way I believe everyone can relate to, regardless of religious affiliation.

You could pretty much sum up my advice this way: Being in a marriage without God is like showering without soap. You can do it, but the result won't be nearly as satisfying.

As you know, marriage is about sharing your life with someone else. The moment you say, "I do," you will have joined forces with another human being and will presumably create new human beings. And when you do, life will no longer be about you. In fact, *your* needs will be last on the list.

Previous generations didn't struggle with sacrifice as much as we do; it was simply a given. They were bound by the universal moral order; religion was an integral part of life; and people didn't have the distractions they do today—the ones that pull us away from a life of sacrifice, toward a life of self-fulfillment.

We may consider it a boon that technology has made life easy, but it has a huge downside in that it pulls us farther and farther away from sacrifice. And sacrifice, or doing for others, is the only path to happiness. That is where true satisfaction lies.

When we ignore this fact, we're left with a void. "Happiness is not a solitary endeavor; it's a joint enterprise, something that can only be created by the whole. Contentment arises from a sense of family, community, and connectedness. Such virtues are in dwindling supply in America," wrote John Perry Barlow in *Forbes*.[83]

Consider the messages women have absorbed about how to have a happy life. "Put yourself first." "Be empowered." "Don't lose yourself in marriage." "Never lower your standards."

Do you think God would say any of these things?

No wonder the modern generation is chronically dissatisfied—sacrifice escapes them. Without God and religion, which are ultimately about sacrifice, we humans would merely exist alongside each other, with no sense of obligation. The ability to give without recognition, to sacrifice, is what marriage is all about. And it's *very* hard to do this without God.

Sadly, faith and religion have taken a nosedive. It is rare to find a wedding today in which God takes center stage—people today are getting married by friends or family who've been ordained. But have you noticed that at the same time religion has declined, lasting love has become more elusive than ever?

Marriage is about learning how to love unconditionally. Without this commitment, life is a just a series of hellos and good-byes. That's where God comes in.

It is impossible to love someone, *really* love someone, without God. Because to love is to put yourself last, to give rather than to get. Humans are weak and selfish by nature, and the presence of God makes us less so.

A recent study by the Chronicle of Philanthropy found that residents in states where religious participation is higher than the rest of the nation gave the greatest percentage of their discretionary income to charity. Indeed, every person I know who lacks faith—

and I admit I don't know a ton—is inherently self-centered: They can't think outside their own wants and needs.

When that's the case, love is impossible.

There's also this. It is not a coincidence that at the same time life became infinitely easier, love became exponentially harder. When life is good, as it has been for decades, faith ceases to be necessary.

Faith kicks in only when life gets difficult or when bad things happen. But technology and a booming economy has made life easy. The modern generation has grown up in an age of abundance; they have no idea what it means to sacrifice or to do without.

When it comes to lasting love, faith is crucial. *The difference in the worldviews of someone who has faith and someone who lacks faith is huge.* Faith, or a lack thereof, is the prism through which we view the world and the people in it. If two people don't agree on this matter, they're going to have a hard time building a life together.

When I was dating my ex, I thought he and I were of one mind on this subject since it seemed to us we'd been raised similarly. Both our mothers were raised Catholic but ultimately rejected that religion. There also wasn't much praying going on in either household. At least not openly.

But there were plenty of differences I didn't see. Unlike me, my ex was never baptized and never went to church. I was baptized Presbyterian, and my family went to church on Easter and Christmas and sporadically throughout the year. I even graduated from Catholic school. (That's a long story . . .) Suffice it to say, I've never *not* believed in God. I've never even questioned His existence.

But my ex was agnostic. Whenever I'd bring up God or church, he'd become visibly uncomfortable. In fact, when we first met, I was still mourning the death of a four-year-old girl I had babysat every week since she was born. I remember wanting to go to church every year on her birthday and asking my ex to go with me, but he'd always refuse. At the time I read this as lack of support, which of course it was. What didn't register was its significance.

My ex was so utterly removed from God and faith that he couldn't even bring himself to *enter* a church.

His discomfort with God and religion bothered me; but because he wasn't hateful about it—on the contrary, he was envious of people of faith—I wasn't concerned. Plus I wasn't thinking about marriage during the early years of our courtship, so I didn't pay much attention to it. But later, when we got engaged, conversations about church would come up and once again he'd get uncomfortable. I remember bringing him to the church in my hometown where we were to be married and he was like a fish out of water.

All those years we were together, I was keenly aware of my ex's indifference toward ethical matters. He had no clear sense of right and wrong, and eventually, I put two and two together. It was because he didn't believe in God. He lacked faith.

Faith is the anchor that keeps us grounded in the face of life's hardships and unexplained phenomena. If you don't have faith in anything other than yourself and the physical world, selfishness is a given and life is meaningless. Without God, people struggle to make sense of things, and they never feel content or satisfied. The physical world leaves people feeling lost and longing for more. The spiritual world fills us up.

There's another reason your marriage needs God: children. Your kids are going to have questions, such as "How did we get here?" Children need something other than their parents to believe in, which becomes even more clear the older children get.

If you're anything like me and your religious background was sketchy, my suggestion is to marry a man of faith. My husband is Catholic and has a strong faith. That we both attended Catholic schools explains why we're of the same mind, but that's not to say we always agree. The important thing is that one partner takes the religious lead. In my marriage, that person is my husband.

I'm not suggesting that in order to be a good person you have to be religious. Many people have a Kantian or Ayn Rand-esque view of the world, a philosophy that defends personal responsibility and a general "do unto others" approach to life. The only problem with it is that it's difficult to impart this philosophy to children.

Teaching faith in God and taking part in daily prayer helps children endure things they cannot understand. It also helps them rely on someone other than Mom and Dad, which is important since their parents aren't always going to be there. Children need to learn that people grow by surviving life's hardships—this is the core of our physical journey. Parents who have faith and use prayer teach children the tools they need to overcome difficult times and appreciate life's gifts.

Once again, modern culture has failed you in this regard, which is why (once again) you'll have to ignore the culture and live an examined life. Had you been born earlier, you would have known a different world, one where God was assumed to be an essential part of everyday life. You would have had a clear and undeniable anchor.

You may laugh about this (you wouldn't be the first), but my husband and I raised our children on a steady diet of *Little House on the Prairie* and *The Waltons*. We did this because the lessons these programs impart—hard work, respect for family, and *love of God*—are timeless and universal. No matter which day and age we live in, such messages matter.

But they're not going to be taught in our culture. Which means if you want your children to know God, you have to know Him yourself. If you don't, they likely won't either.

At the end of the day, faith means believing in something bigger than yourself. It means accepting that you are not the center of the universe.

God is.

LEARN A FEW BASICS ABOUT BEING A WIFE

Well, we're almost there. Now that you know how to think counterculturally and make smart decisions that bring love into your life, it's time to focus on what it means to be married. What do *you* have to offer *him*?

I don't know if you've thought about marriage in these terms, but it's critical you do if you want to be successfully hitched. There is an art to being a wife—and trust me, I still haven't mastered it. I'm always learning something new, and I've been a wife for decades!

That's the thing about marriage. It is a continual act of refinement: your learning how to be a better wife, and his learning how to be a better husband. None of us is born with these skills. So allow me to share a few things I've learned the hard way, the most important of which is this:

Unless you married a man who lacks character, what *you* bring to the marriage table will likely determine the fate of your marriage. In other words, it's not what your guy can do for you but what you can do for your guy that matters. That's the attitude you need going forward.

Now before you charge back with, "What? Why should the strength of my marriage fall on my shoulders? Doesn't my husband have a role to play?"

He does. But the male/female dance has a specific choreography; and the sooner you learn it, the better off you'll be. Wives have always been the arbiters of sex and relationships. As was the case when you were dating, your attitude and behavior really do set the stage.

This is in part because men respond to women out of a desire to see their wives happy. Which means if you treat your man like a king, you'll be treated in return like a queen. Treat him poorly, and he'll either bite or walk away.

The other reason to stay focused on yourself is because you can only control yourself. You can't force a man to be what you want him to be or to do what you want him to do—not without serious ramifications. But you *can* learn how to bring out the best in him so that he wants to do better. Now that's power!

So with that in mind, below are my top six tricks of the trade when it comes to being a wife. They'll probably sound foreign to you at first. But once you've embraced them and put them to action—and then see the results—they'll begin to make all the sense in the world.

1. Dump your feminist mind.

The Food Network's Ree Drummond, aka The Pioneer Woman, wrote a memoir in 2012 called *The Pioneer Woman: Black Heels to Tractor Wheels—A Love Story*.[84] In it, Ree explains that she was born in Oklahoma but moved to California to go to college, where she soaked up her vegetarian, freewheelin' lifestyle like a sponge.

After graduation, Ree's career took off, and getting married and having babies were the last things on her mind. But on her way back from Los Angeles, en route to Chicago, she stopped in her hometown, where she met a devastatingly masculine cowboy she calls "Marlboro Man." A relationship ensued, and eventually Marlboro Man asked Ree to marry him.

A rancher with deep roots in the land he works, he had no intention of leaving his ranch—so Ree decided to give up her independent, footloose life in the big city to become a rancher's wife. Today, the Pioneer Woman and her Marlboro Man have four children together, and her freewheelin' days are behind her.

The reason I'm sharing her story is because throughout the book, Ree makes several references to her formerly feminist self. More than once, she wrote about how she had to get of rid of the feminist thoughts that had invaded her mind. The ones that told her she shouldn't give up her dreams for a man and that she should never fall for a strapping fella and rearrange her entire life plans as a result. Strong, powerful women don't swoon.

Yet swoon Ree did, and the sexual energy she describes as a result of surrendering her feminist disposition was palpable. Ree's life was in no way restricted as a result of marriage and motherhood. On the contrary, she cobbled together a career she could pursue alongside her role as a wife and mother.

Ree's story is a fantastic illustration of how feminism pulls women away from their natural feminine instincts and steers them toward a false notion of empowerment. There really is a different way to move through the world as a woman. (See Step #3.)

2. Put down your sword.

Dumping your feminist mind won't be easy, since the equality narrative you've absorbed claims women have been subjugated for decades due to an unfair playing field. As a result, it is now second nature for women to ward off men who they're convinced hold them down so there's nothing left but some half-baked version of a former self.

Due to this (wrong-headed) assumption, sexual equality is considered the antidote to the oppression women purportedly endure—which causes women to feel they need to prove they're just as strong and capable as a man. To them, this represents power.

In reality, all women end up doing is proving to men how angry they are. And who wants to be with someone who's mad all the time?

As a result of this narrative about men and marriage, modern marriages and relationships amount to little more than a power struggle. They're competitive, rather than complementary. The glorious differences between the sexes that allow love to flourish have been obliterated, and in its place are anger and strife that manifests itself in a complete lack of polarity.

Polarity is vital for love to thrive. Without it, a relationship goes nowhere. The definition of polarity is "the state of having two opposite or contradictory tendencies, opinions, or aspects." Since women have been encouraged to become like men in their attempt to achieve so-called equality, polarity in relationships has vanished. Rather than one man and one woman, there are effectively two men vying for the same role.

Women have also been groomed to be suspicious of men, which would naturally cause any woman to have her guard up.

What if I told you that everything you've been taught about men and marriage is wrong? What if, when it comes to love, you've been moving through the world with the wrong map?

In fact, you have.

If you want lasting love, the very first thing you have to do is put down your sword and start to assume the best, rather than the worst, of men. Because the truth is, men are the exact opposite of what you've been told.

Far from being oppressors, when treated well a man is a woman's greatest supporter. He wants to see you thrive. He wants to see you happy. He will even take a back seat to your wants and desires. But only if you treat him well.

If you view him as the enemy, you'll get nothing in return.

3. Be sweet.

The third thing you'll need to learn how to do is to be sweet. So many relationships could be salvaged if women were simply *nicer* to men.

Here again women have been sold a bill of goods. They've been conditioned to believe that being sweet means being weak, which has resulted in a generation of, for lack of a better word, bitches.

It wasn't that long ago that being bitchy was considered a negative trait, but today it's considered a positive one. Countless movies and television programs associate female strength with bitchiness. There was even a book published in 2002 called *Why Men Love Bitches*, which was very successful. The author, Sherry Argov, argued that being a bitch is the opposite of being a doormat.

Being a bitch is *not* the opposite of being a doormat. Being a doormat means being unable to stand up for yourself and letting people walk all over you. The alternative is not to be a "bitch," which means to be aggressive, demanding, and difficult, or to run roughshod over everyone. It's to gain the confidence you need to stand up for yourself when necessary, which can done while being nice. They're not mutually exclusive.

So much of the confusion about female strength is a result of people's perception that the traditional housewife was a doormat. (Hence the theme of *Why Men Love Bitches*: down with the dumb housewife, up with the empowered woman who doesn't take crap from a man.) But the housewives of the past, as a rule, weren't doormats. That narrative was simply infused into every book and film you've absorbed your entire life for the purpose of selling an agenda. It isn't real.

Those supposedly hapless housewives understood men and marriage and knew how to navigate marriage in a way modern women don't. I'm sure you've heard the phrase, "You'll attract more bees with honey than you will with vinegar." This is the aspect of human nature against which feminists have rebelled. To them, being sweet means being a doormat.

They are wrong. Being feminine—or being kind, soft, and nurturing—would only be suffocating if you were in love with a Neanderthal who walked around saying "Get me a beer, Woman!" But you know what? I've never actually met a Neanderthal, and I'm in my fifties! I'm sure he exists somewhere on the planet, but he isn't the norm, or I would have met him by now. Most men are nothing like that.

Do you remember the 2012 movie theater massacre when a man named James Holmes murdered twelve people (and injured fifty-eight more) in Aurora, Colorado? Three men—Jon Blunk, Matt McQuinn, and Alex Teves—died shielding their girlfriends from Holmes's rampage.[85]

Those three men, not James Holmes, represent the average man in America.

A man's desire to love, honor, and protect women is instinctive. And this is largely due to their inherent respect and love for women. But men will not come to the defense of a bitch because they're too busy having to defend themselves *from* her.

Men, in other words, don't love bitches. They love nice women. Sweet women. Gentle women. Kind women. Affectionate women. Maternal women.

Those are the kind of women who get the best of men. Do you want to be one of them or don't you?

4. Surrender control.

When it comes to being a wife, deference is key. *Deference* means a courteous regard for, or respect toward, another person's opinions or judgment.

You probably haven't heard this term before, at least with respect to relationships since modern women aren't encouraged to be deferential. They think it means being subservient to men—and if there's one thing women today pride themselves on, it's being in charge and in control. They want to drive the car, rather than be driven.

When channeled properly, in the workforce for example, this quality can work well. But in love it's a complete disaster.

In any marriage or relationship, only one person can lead. The man doesn't *always* have to be the driver; but in most cases, that's what works. I know putting it in these terms riles people's feathers. But surrendering control of the wheel does not mean being "less than."

Now I tend to be a control freak. Simply put, I like things the way I like them—and if I want something done right, I prefer to do it myself. This has worked well for me in my life and my career, but not in my marriage. Here's an example.

For a long time I would tell my husband how to drive, and he couldn't stand it. It caused a lot of conflict. Once I surrendered this habit—and it took a while, believe me—everything changed. I no longer tell my husband how to drive, so there are no longer any fights in the car. He still takes the long way to get somewhere, which was the main source of contention, but I honestly no longer care. Since I couldn't change him, I changed me—and that's what made the difference.

In fact, I *love* being a passenger now! If I'm feeling really crazy, I leave my purse at home because that makes me feel even less in control! As a self-employed person, I'm in charge of everything all the time. When I'm with my husband, I don't want to be in charge. So I surrender.

Another problem that arises in marriages in which two people try to take charge is the need to be right. But needing to be right for the sake of being right is the opposite of love. In fact, needing to be in control in general is just fear manifesting itself in an ugly manner.

But if you choose a good man, your ability to surrender will be rewarded. You husband isn't going to hurt you, walk all over you, or control you. Rather, he will take care of you and your needs. Men don't like to fight with women—and when two people try to drive the bus, that's what happens. That's why you need to surrender.

Sadly, modern women have no tools for this dynamic—no clue how to step back and let men be in charge. To them, the mere idea sounds appalling. That's because they've been taught that *not* being in control means losing one's identity or becoming a doormat.

It doesn't.

5. Have more sex, not less.

"Ours is now a terribly under-sexed society. I have talked to a lot of young women about this, and they just don't seem to do it anymore. Honestly. I suppose it's because we all have so many other demands on our time now."[86] So says romance novelist Jilly Cooper.

Married sex has indeed taken a nosedive. I'm reminded of a conversation I had with a woman I know named Laura. Laura is a forty-nine-year-old physical therapist. She's petite, with long, wavy, dark hair and beautiful skin—think Giada De Laurentiis. She told me that not one but *several* of her friends confided in her that they rarely sleep with their husbands. There was nothing wrong with these men, she said—they were great husbands, and not unattractive or overweight. Their wives just didn't feel like having sex and didn't think they should have to.

Laura was despondent upon hearing this and didn't know what to say. Should she tell her friends how wrong that is? She wasn't sure. She and I had a long conversation about what's going on with relationships these days. When I told Laura how so many women are mired in the me-first, empowered feminist worldview that suggests caring for a man equates to weakness in a woman, it confounded her. It's so easy to take care of a husband, she said. What's the problem? Just be nice, cook, and have sex!

A marriage counselor I know once told me that when she was a guest on *Oprah*, one of the husbands on the panel expressed dismay over his wife's weight gain and admitted he was less attracted to her. Thus, they weren't having sex.

When my counselor friend (a woman) supported the husband's request that his wife lose weight, she practically got her head cut off. Both Oprah and the audience told her how terrible it was that she would suggest a wife lose weight in order to be more attractive to her husband. That the counselor said husbands should do the same didn't matter.

The implication was clear: Women should be able to let themselves go, and their husbands should just get over it. Any other attitude amounts to oppression.

People embrace this same victim mentality when husbands have affairs, even though when husbands cheat they're usually suffering in the marriage just as wives are when *they* cheat. The difference is that when husbands cheat, they're publicly chastised. When wives cheat, it's assumed their husbands drove them to it.

Yes, some men cheat (just as some women do); and more often than not, husbands stray because they feel rejected by their wives. But we're not allowed to acknowledge this because it means we're blaming the woman for her husband's transgression—even though addressing the *reasons* he strayed would clearly resolve the underlying problem!

To even imply that wives play a part in why husbands stray borders on blasphemy. But the truth is, every action has a reaction. Rather than view it as "husband perpetrator/wife victim," we should ask ourselves what went wrong in the first place.

It's important to note, too, that men and women cheat for different reasons. Husbands often cheat when the opportunity presents itself (remember: men can separate sex from emotion), and they haven't had sex with their wives in a long time. For wives, the circumstances are a bit different. "By the time a woman is at the point of physically cheating with another man, she has often emotionally vacated her primary relationship," writes sex therapist Ian Kerner.[87] When this happens, women can become vulnerable to the first man who starts paying them some attention.

Both scenarios (why men cheat and why women cheat) stem from the same issue—a desire to be loved and accepted—but their means of connection differ. A man's primary mode of communication is sex—morning, noon, and night.

Speaking his language works. *Every time.*

6. Talk less; listen more.

Communication is often hailed as The Answer to a great relationship. But talking is overrated.

I agree that communication is key in that you shouldn't hold back your feelings; otherwise you'll blow up later. But there's such a thing as too much talking. In fact, there are going to be plenty of times in your marriage when the best thing you can do for your relationship is to just sit there and be quiet and not say a thing.

Silence is so powerful. When I say nothing as opposed to something, I often find I've said a lot. In my case, being the talker I am, and considering what I do for a living, my husband's so used to hearing what I think that my silence is uber-powerful.

Think about a time when your guy said something that embarrassed you. When this happens, the urge to speak can be overwhelming. But if you can muster the courage—the *deference*—to keep still, trust me: you will have spoken volumes.

Most men know what their wives or girlfriends are thinking because we talk so much more than they do. As a result, they sometimes tune us out. This is annoying, I know, but it also means that when we don't say anything, they hear that silence loud and clear. (Sort of like when men finally *do* say something, we women perk up!)

So when I say communication is overrated, I don't mean you should hold all your thoughts and feelings inside and never let them out.

I just mean sometimes you should.

One obvious advantage to not talking so much is you become a better listener. You also have the opportunity to collect your thoughts before speaking.

I never used to collect my thoughts—I spoke them. If I didn't like something, I'd say so. If I was feeling frustrated or tired, I'd announce it. If I had an opinion (and I always have an opinion), I'd share it. Basically, every thought and feeling I had used to be spoken. My feelings were a faucet.

I cannot tell you how long it took me to get it and how hard it was, at first, to stop talking so much. But eventually, I did. And I learned how powerful silence can be.

Try it.

So that's my best "quick read" advice about being a wife. If you want more in-depth information, pick up a copy of either of my books, *The Alpha Female's Guide to Men & Marriage* or *Women Who Win at Love.*

In the meantime, keep in mind that being married is a work in progress and requires a great deal of maturity and self-reflection. Whatever you do, just know you have a central role to play in the health of your marriage and of the direction it goes. To resolve whatever issues arise, you must be able to look in the mirror. If you cannot do this, you will fail.

Anger, self-righteousness, and entitlement have no place in marriage. If you want love to last, you need to learn a man's language. The words you speak to him—and just as importantly, the *way* you speak them—will either breathe life into a man or they will cut him to the core. That's the power you have as a woman.

There. I've now provided you with the advice and information no one ever gave you about men and marriage. The question is, what will you do with it?

Endnotes

PART ONE

1   Eric Klinenberg, "One's a Crowd," *The New York Times*, February 4, 2012.

2   Lena Dunham to Frank Bruni, "The Bleaker Sex," *The New York Times*, March 31, 2012.

3   Hanna Rosin, "Sexual Freedom and Women's Success," *The Wall Street Journal*, March 23, 2012.

4   Janelle Nanos, "Single by Choice: Why More of Us Than Ever Before Are Happy to Never Get Married," *Boston Magazine*, January 2012.

CHAPTER 1

5   Gloria Steinem, "Gloria in Her Own Words," HBO documentary, August 2011.

6   Brad LaRosa, "Sandra Bullock Ribs Street on Rivalry," ABC News, March 4, 2010.

CHAPTER 2

7   Suzanne Venker, "Rich Women and Emasculated Men," *National Review*, April 2, 2012, http://www.nationalreview.com/home-front/295021/rich-women-and-emasculated-men/suzanne-venker.

CHAPTER 3

8   Mike Nguyen, "Jordan Peterson VICE Interview (FULL) The Missing Parts", Youtube video, 17:01, February 18, 2018, https://www.youtube.com/watch?v=S-9dZSlUjVls.

9   Mary Matalin, *Letters to My Daughters* (New York: Simon & Schuster, 2004), 45.

10   Tom Valeo, "Boy brain, meet girl brain," Tampabay.com, August 6, 2006, http://www.sptimes.com/2006/08/06/news_pf/Books/Boy_brain__meet_girl_.shtml.

11   Lawrence Spivak to Gloria Steinem, NBC News *Meet the Press*, September 10, 1972.

CHAPTER 4

12   Laurie Wagner, *Expectations* (San Francisco: Chronicle Books, 1998), 33.

13 Anne-Marie Slaughter, "Women Still Can't Have It All," *The Atlantic*, July/August 2012.

PART TWO

STEP #1

14 Gordon MacDonald, *Ordering Your Private World* (Nashville: Thomas Nelson, 2007).

15 Ibid.

16 Myrna Blyth, *Spin Sisters: How the Women of the Media Sell Unhappiness and Liberalism to the Women of America* (New York: St. Martin's Press, 2004), vii.

17 Dani Klein Modisett, "My Kids Stole My Ambition!" *Huffington Post*, February 2, 2012.

18 Steve Jobs, commencement address, Stanford University (Stanford, CA), 2005.

STEP #2

19 Jone Johnson Lewis, "Julia Child Quotes," About.com: Women's History, http:// womenshistory.about.com/od/juliachild/a/julia_child_2.htm.

20 Charles R. Swindoll, ThinkExist.com Quotations, http://thinkexist.com/quotation/ life_is_what_happens_to_you_and_how_you_react_to/158456.html.

21 Barry Schwartz, *The Paradox of Choice: Why More Is Less* (New York: Harper Collins, 2004), 142.

22 Rachel Lehmann-Haupt, "The Aniston Syndrome," Babble, July 19, 2010, http:// www.babble.com/pregnancy/gettingpregnant.

23 Ibid.

24 Ibid.

25 Second Acts, "Chef's Special: Cooking and Cruising," *The Wall Street Journal*, July 12, 2012, http:// online.wsj.com/article/SB10001424052702304840904577426544 065238990.html.

26 Charles Murray, "Why Capitalism Has an Image Problem," *The Wall Street Journal*, July 30, 2012.

27 David McCullough Jr., "David McCullough Jr.'s commencement address: You're Not Special," *Boston Herald*, June 7, 2012, http://bostonherald.com/news/regional/ view/20120607youre_ not_special.

STEP #3

28 Kris Fuchs, "Letting Go of the BlackBerry," *The Wall Street Journal*, March 27, 2012.

29 Louann Brizendine, *The Female Brain* (New York: Broadway Books, 2006), 12.

30   Ibid.

31   Kenneth Minogue, "Modern Love," *The Wall Street Journal*, March 10, 2012.

32   Wikiquote, s.v. "My Big Fat Greek Wedding," http://en.wikiquote.org/wiki/My_Big_Fat_Greek_Wedding.

33   Steve Harvey, *Act Like a Lady, Think Like a Man* (New York: Harper Collins, 2009), 180–81.

34   Sam Botta, interview with author. (May 2012)

35   Harvey, *Act Like a Lady*, 43.

36   See Brizendine, *The Female Brain*, [[insert page numbers; if this point is actually from both her books, add that

37   Step #4

Scarlett Online, *Gone with the Wind* Script Two, http://www.scarlettonline.com/gone_with_the_wind_script_2.htm.

38   Maureen Dowd, "An Ideal Husband," *The New York Times*, July 26, 2008.

39   M. Scott Peck, *The Road Less Traveled* (New York: Simon & Schuster, 1978), 84.

40   Ibid., 85.

41   Ibid., 15.

STEP #5

42   Meg Jay, "The Downside of Cohabiting before Marriage," *The New York Times* Sunday Review (opinion pages), April 12, 2012, http://www.nytimes.com/2012/04/15/opinion/sunday/the-downside-of-cohabiting-before-marriage.html?pagewanted=all.

43   David Popenoe, "Cohabitation: The Marriage Enemy," *USA Today*, July 28, 2000.

44   Jay, "The Downside of Cohabiting before Marriage."

45   Schwartz, *The Paradox of Choice*, 228; emphasis added. (See Step #2, n. 3.)

46   George Gilder, *Men and Marriage* (Gretna, LA: Pelican Publishing, 1992), 187–88.

STEP #6

47   Megan Rutherford, "When Mother Stays Home," *Time.com*, October 16, 2000, http://www.time.com/time/magazine/article/0,9171,998242,00.html.

48   Harvey, *Act Like a Lady*, 11. (See Step #1, n. 5.)

49   Liza Mundy, *The Richer Sex: How the New Majority of Female Breadwinners Is Transforming Sex, Love, and Family* (New York: Simon & Schuster, 2012), 2.

50   http://www.thefreedictionary.com/empower.

STEP #7

51 Rachel Weight, "How *The Notebook* Has Ruined Me," *The Huffington Post*, May 11, 2012, http://www.huffingtonpost.com/rachel-weight/the-notebook_b_1508359.html.

52 Po Bronson and Ashley Merryman, *Nurtureshock: New Thinking about Children* (New York: Twelve, 2009), 9.

53 Vicki Larson, "Why Women Walk Out More Than Men," *The Huffington Post*, January 24, 2011, http://www.huffingtonpost.com/vicki-larson/why-women-want-out-more-t_b_792133.html.

54 Schwartz, *The Paradox of Choice.* (see Step #2, n 3.)

55 Ibid., 229.

STEP #8

56 Human Fertilisation and Embryology Authority, "Fertility Facts and Figures 2008," December 8, 2010, http://www.hfea.gov.uk/docs/2010-12-08_Fertility_Facts_and_Figures_2008_Publication_PDF.PDF, 10.

57 Ibid.

58 Rebecca Walker, "How my mother's fanatical views tore us apart," *Mail Online* (UK), May 23, 2008, http://www.dailymail.co.uk/femail/ article-1021293/ How-mothers-fanatical-feminist-views-tore-apart- daughter-The-Color-Purple-author.html.

59 Miriam Grossman, "The Dangers of Social Ideology in Campus Health Care," *Policy Express*, no. 7-2, April 15, 2007, Clare Boothe Luce Policy Institute.

60 "Movie and TV Stars Become Mommies after 40," Squidoo, n.d. http://www.squidoo.com/Over40celebritymoms; accessed August 28, 2012.

61 "Brooke Shields: an advocate for fertility issues," Toronto Centre for Advanced Reproductive Technology, n.d., http://bodyandhealth.canada.com/channel_health_features_details.asp?health_feature_id=378&article_id=1200&channel_id=2048&relation_id=36904; accessed August 28, 2012.

62 Associated Press, "Courteney Cox Has Baby Girl," FoxNews.com, June 14, 2004, http://www.foxnews.com/story/0,2933,122604,00.html.

63 "Movie and TV Stars Become Mommies after 40."

64 Kate Fridkis, "The Invisible Baby That Follows Me Around," *Eat the Damn Cake* (blog), December 16, 2011, http://www.eatthedamncake.com/2011/12/16/the-invisible-baby-that-follows-me-around/.

STEP #9

65 Jennifer Lopez, "Jennifer Lopez Talks Adoption, Life as a Single Mom and Having More Kids," *E! Online*, May 9, 2012.

66   Erica Komisar, "The Human Cost of Sweden's Welfare State," *The Wall Street Journal*, July 11, 2018, https://www.wsj.com/articles/the-human-cost-of-swedens-welfare-state-1531346908.

67   William and Wendy Dreskin, *The Daycare Decision* (New York: M. Evans and Company, Inc., 1983), 50.

68   Kitty Kelley, *Oprah: A Biography* (New York: Crown Publishers, 2010), 160.

69   Karl Zinsmeister, "The Problem with Daycare," *American Enterprise*, May/June 1998.

70   Nancy Gibbs, "What Women Want Now," *Time*, October 14, 2009.

71   Betsey Stevenson and Justin Wolfers, *The Paradox of Declining Female Happiness* (Working Paper 14969) (Cambridge, MA: National Bureau of Economic Research, 2009), http://www.nber.org/papers/w14969.pdf?new_window=1, p. 5.

72   "Transcript and Video of Speech by Sheryl Sandberg, Chief Operating Officer, Facebook," Barnard College commencement, New York City, May 17, 2011, http://barnard.edu/headlines/transcript-and-video-speech-sheryl-sandberg-chief-operating-officer-facebook.

73   Ibid.

74   Catharine Smith, "Facebook COO Sheryl Sandberg, 'I Feel Guilty Working Because of My Kids," *Huffington Post*, July 4, 2011, http://www.huffingtonpost.com/2011/07/04/facebook-coo-sheryl-sandberg-new-yorker_n_889768.html.

75   Iris Krasnow, *Surrendering to Motherhood: Losing Your Mind, Finding Your Soul* (New York: Miramax, 1998), 72.

STEP #10

76   Stephanie Chen, "Could you be 'infected' by a friend's divorce?" *CNN Living*, June 10, 2010.

77   Maggie Gallagher, "The New Enemies of Eros," *National Review Online*, October 20, 2011.

78   Schwartz, *The Paradox of Choice*, 228; emphasis added. (See Step #2, n. 3.)

79   Barry Schwartz, "The Paradox of Choice" (talk), TED Conference, July 2005.

80   Ibid.

81   Ibid.

82   Kathleen Kinmont, "The 'Do I Really Need a Man?' Checklist," *HuffPost Divorce*: The Blog, http://www.huffingtonpost.com/kathleen-kinmont/life-after-divorce_b_1478051.html.

STEP #11

83   John Perry Barlow, "The Pursuit of Emptiness: Why Americans Have Never Been a Happy Bunch," *Forbes*, December 3, 2001, 97.

STEP #12

84   Ree Drummond, *The Pioneer Woman: Black Heels to Tractor Wheels—A Love Story*, (New York: William Morrow, 2011).

85   Alex Groberman, "Jon Blunk, Matt McQuinn, Alex Teves Died Trying to Save Girlfriends During Batman Movie Massacre," July 23, 2012, Opposing Views, http://www.opposingviews.com/i/society/crime/jon-blunk-matt-mcquinn-alex-teves-died-trying-save-girlfriends-during-batman-movie.

86   Jilly Cooper, "'Bonkbuster' is dead because women have lost their libidos," *Telegraph* (UK), June 24, 2012.

87   Ian Kerner, "Fox on Sex: Why Women Cheat," September 13, 2010.

ABOUT THE AUTHOR

Author photo by Kelsey Roa

Suzanne Venker is on a mission to deprogram women from the toxic cultural influences that undermine their success in life and in love. She's the author of five books, a certified relationship coach, and host of *The Suzanne Venker Show*. Her work has appeared in countless publications, such as Fox News, the *Washington Examiner*, *TIME*, *USA Today*, and the *New York Post*. She has also appeared on many television and radio programs. Suzanne lives in the Midwest with her husband of twenty-three years. They have a son and a daughter, both of whom are in college. Her website is www.suzannevenker.com and her podcast can be reached at www.thesuzannevenkershow.com.